COMEBACK CAREERS

RETHINK, REFRESH, REINVENT YOUR SUCCESS— AT 40, 50, AND BEYOND

MIKA BRZEZINSKI
GINNY BRZEZINSKI

hachette
BOOKS

NEW YORK   BOSTON

Hachette Books
Hachette Book Group
1290 Avenue of the Americas
New York, NY 10104
hachettebookgroup.com
twitter.com/hachettebooks
instagram.com/hachettebooks

First Edition: January 2020
Hachette Books is a division of Hachette Book Group, Inc.

The Hachette Books name and logo are trademarks of Hachette Book Group, Inc.
The publisher is not responsible for websites (or their content) that are not owned by the publisher.

The Hachette Speakers Bureau provides a wide range of authors for speaking events. To find out more, go to www.hachettespeakersbureau.com or call (866) 376-6591.

Editorial production by Christine Marra, Marrathon Production Services. www.marrathoneditorial.org
Book design by Jane Raese
Set in 12.5-point Adobe Garamond Pro

Library of Congress Cataloging-in-Publication Data has been applied for.

ISBN 978-1-60286-590-7 (hardcover), ISBN 978-1-60286-589-1 (ebook)

Printed in the United States of America

LSC-C

10 9 8 7 6 5 4 3 2 1

CONTENTS

INTRODUCTION

Stronger, Wiser, Better

I used to think my career would be over by the time I hit my forties.

———

EVERYONE IN TELEVISION knows this truth: time is not on your side. My attitude was that I needed to save enough money by the time I turned fifty because then my career would be over. In an industry that values youth and beauty, another birthday often signals another step toward your own expiration date.

But the funny thing is that what I've learned in my forties and beyond is what has prepared me for reinvention. What makes me feel powerful right now is all the knocks I have taken over the past decade. Whether it's being publicly fired and starting my career all over again, or being mocked on social media (by the president of the United States, among countless others), or just everyday failures and frustrations—I've gotten better at taking a punch, I've gotten better at punching back, and I've gotten stronger as a result. I'm far less traumatized when something changes completely and I then have to redevelop a project I've been working on for six months. The daily knocks that you've endured by this point in your life—that's how you develop a thick skin, and it makes all the difference.

So now, as I enter my fifties, I may have some battle scars, but I truly feel like I'm in the prime of my life. I love my work on *Morning Joe*, interviewing some of the most interesting people in the world and addressing big questions about the direction of our country. I've worked my way up (and down and back up) the corporate ladder. I've used my own experience—along with expert advice and research—to write a series of best-selling books that empower women to take control of their careers and maybe even their lives. I am proud of the movement I started with *Know Your Value*, the book I wrote about the forces—both internal and external—that are holding women back in the workplace. It took me so long to truly understand my value, to communicate it effectively, and to get what I deserved—not just money but also recognition, influence, and the power to dictate my own terms. I wanted to empower other women to find their voice and get the raises and promotions they deserve. Know Your Value is now the basis of a women's conference series, a bustling online community, and more. To this day, everywhere I go, women from all walks of life want to talk to me about that book and how its message resonated with them.

All this is to say: this is not what I expected my career or life to look like at my age. Perhaps I was wrong about the limitations I thought I would face. A generation ago a woman like me might be the only woman in the room, if she got there at all. There just weren't a lot of role models of powerful women working and thriving well beyond our life's midpoint. But times have changed. Now we're seeing more. And our runway is extending—Susan Zirinsky taking over CBS at sixty-six, Speaker of the House Nancy Pelosi, incredibly powerful at seventy-nine, and my own mother, still working as an artist at eighty-eight.

These are women who know their value and are shattering all kinds of ceilings and stereotypes about women and power. Their age and experience are assets, not liabilities.

Midlife doesn't have to be a career killer for women after all . . . right?

———

It's seven o'clock on a cold morning in December 2016. I'm on set talking about Donald Trump's surprise victory, which, though a month old, still boggles everyone's mind. I've been up since 3:30 a.m. as usual—hair, makeup, six newspapers, and coffee—and we've been at it for an hour. The bright lights on set, combined with my early-morning wake-up call, make it seem like it's noon. Someone on set brings up Know Your Value, and I am thrilled because my Know Your Value movement is on a roll. NBCUniversal is rolling out conferences nationwide with me—we are bringing my empowerment message to working women around the country, and I am feeling great.

Then my phone buzzes. It's a text from my sister-in-law Ginny.

Hey Mika—Can KYV address women like me who downshifted to take care of kids and now want to pivot careers or return to work? We have value too!

This came as a bit of a bubble-bursting shock. It had never dawned on me that my own sister-in-law and many other women felt left out by Know Your Value.

I realized in that moment that so much of my attention had been on women who were in the first half of their careers, struggling to move up. But what about midcareer women, women in their forties and fifties, and, especially, women who aren't currently working—women who had been laid off, or were trying to pivot to something new, or had off-ramped or back-burnered their careers because of the often-incompatible demands of caregiving and work? I know very well what it feels like to be going through a career change and to wonder whether I have any value at all. How could I address these women, help them feel fierce, help them take control over their work life?

Slightly bruised ego aside, I realized immediately that this was something I needed to address as we continued to expand Know Your Value. Clearly, because my employment had been pretty steady in recent years, I also needed a trusted, talented ally with firsthand experience to help me reach women returning to or transitioning in the workforce. As fast as my fingers could type, I replied *YES!* and asked Ginny to take on the project: Create a new silo for Know Your Value. Become the Know Your Value voice for this group of women. Be our Comeback Career blogger. And, of course, write a book with me. This was an opportunity to help Know Your Value reach out to the many women out there who were feeling just like Ginny and to shine a spotlight on the challenges they face and the value they possess.

And so that December day *Comeback Careers* was born.

———

GINNY AND I SPENT the next year and more working on this project, digging deep into the subject of women at midlife, their careers, and how to articulate the special value a seasoned woman can bring to new ventures. We interviewed scores of women who have taken career breaks, transitioned, or started something entirely new at midlife. We talked to career-transition experts and coaches. We asked the critical question: How can women past the midpoint of their lives make this part of their careers the best part?

We began by focusing on moms like Ginny who were returning to work after a career break or downshift. We found that she was far from alone, that time-outs, downshifts, gigs, pivots, and work-arounds are necessary features—not bugs—in many women's career trajectories. Today close to 30 percent of women report that at some point they have taken a significant (more than a two-year) career break to care for family (children, parents, spouse). Statistics show that the overwhelming majority who take time off will want to return to the workforce. After three or ten or even twenty years, when the work-life balance becomes easier or the kids are in school, or when the nest is emptying and the tuition bills are exploding, or when divorce or illness or even the death of a spouse brings loss of the family income, many women want and need to reboot their careers or forge a new career path—but they aren't sure how to make their next move.

We quickly discovered it's not just the stay-at-home moms and downshifters who need a hand with a career reboot. There's a whole midlife career crisis going on for scores of women in their forties and fifties. In our conversations with these women we heard the word "invisible" a few too many times. Midlife is a time of numerous life transitions, many of them difficult, painful, and frustrating. Turns out that there are a whole lot of women—not just the women who took a career break—who today are trying to figure out their value and career path at midlife.

The truth is that knowing your value is more complicated as you get older. Sure, by now you probably have a track record of experience—you know what you're good at and, as my friend and former senator Claire McCaskill says, "you have receipts to prove it." You have more patience, deeper networks, more practical knowledge. You're at the apex of your capabilities. You should be killing it. But just as women at midlife should be celebrating their strength, for so many of them the ground starts to shift under their feet. Sometimes their own values and priorities have shifted: what seemed important in the first half of their careers—glamour, travel, making that career-defining win—now seems less compelling. Sometimes they feel that their momentum at work has cooled, though not by choice, or that they've been sidelined altogether. And whether or not they would put a name to it, most women around age fifty operate under the convergence of gender bias and age bias. Their jobs are more insecure. *They* are more insecure.

Ginny and I wondered: How can we help women rewrite this narrative, take control of their careers, and make this a time of acceleration toward meaning and, while we're at it, money? How can they operate from a power position instead of feeling increasingly vulnerable?

It seems like just last week we were freaking out about our ticking biological clocks. Now it's our career clocks that we can't stop hearing. Whether you're a "fired at fifty" or the collateral damage of a corporate reorganization, you hear that clock. Maybe you heard that ticking when you hit a milestone birthday and said, "There is no way I can do this f*&king job for the next couple of decades." Or your nest empties and your purpose leaves the house and you are ready to write your next chapter but don't know how to start. Or you are trying to come up with a viable side hustle because you are worried sick about whether you've saved enough for retirement. Or you are simply looking for more meaning and fulfillment in life and have the skills and talent but are afraid you're too old to try something new—and that damn clock just keeps ticking.

We see you, and we're here to help.

It's time for a Know Your Value intervention.

These years can be the best of your life, and that's not just my own personal experience. In our research we talked to many women who told us exactly that. Their enthusiasm came as a bit of a shock after all the angst-ridden testimony we'd heard from women who hadn't taken steps to launch their own comeback career. The women who were thriving had started businesses after forty-five, gone back to school, reinvented themselves, returned to work after career breaks. They used terms like *stronger, wiser, badass,* and *primetime* to reassess their midlife from a new perspective.

We're going to help you get *your* groove back too.

I've spent a decade telling women that if they want a raise or a promotion, they need to know and be able to articulate their value. It worked for thousands of women, and it is a message that women in the second half of their careers need to hear as well.

You are stronger, wiser, and better at the midpoint. You have skills, experience, and maturity, and you need to tap into that power. We are going to show you how.

I believe that if you can identify and articulate your value, you can rebound from any setback or career break into a new, more fulfilling career—whether you are thirty-five or sixty. Knowing your value is the key. Finding work that you love will make you happier, more fulfilled, and more financially secure. It will put you back in control.

We wrote this book for you. We wanted to create a guidebook to help women rediscover and learn how to show their value, to reboot their confidence, and to figure out a new path. It's the book I wish I'd had when I was fired and sitting at home, trying to figure out my next move.

It's all here.

With this book we will help you rewire your mindset and create your action plan for getting to the next chapter. You'll find résumé strategies, social media advice, dos and don'ts for interviewing, negotiating guidance, and recommendations to ensure that your digital footprint complements your IRL (in real life) goals.

We'll show you how networking now is as much about brainstorming with your girlfriends over coffee or wine as it is about making awkward small talk with strangers at conferences. Having a "squad" at midlife to seek in-person support and guidance from is now more important than ever. Let the women in your life power charge your next steps. We'll show you how.

We tackle the issue of ageism and get the best advice for combating its many forms. We've got advice for working in today's multigenerational workplace—where your boss and many colleagues may be decades younger.

Beyond advice, inspiration, and an action plan, at the end of the book we've listed more than a hundred resources to help with your return, reinvention, or rebound—from websites that detail mid-career re-entry programs, to resources with support for starting your own business, to the new crop of women's freelance job boards and free online class sites to power up your tech skills.

We won't tell you that this journey will be easy or painless. But from our experience working on this project, what we will tell you is that returning, reinventing, or rebooting a career is eminently possible. Getting started is half the battle. One woman who successfully returned after eighteen years out of work told us, "Fear was my biggest obstacle. When I got past that, I was all set."

As women, we're fierce when it comes to protecting, defending, and amplifying the success of others. We go to the mat for our spouses, our children, and our colleagues. But when it comes to knowing, articulating, and defending our own value, we go silent. Or we self-deprecate and apologize our way through the conversation.

That changes today.

Read this guide, mark it up, dog-ear the pages, do a deep dive into the Resources. Whether you are headed back to familiar business terrain or considering a pivot to a new career, whether this is about the paycheck or the fulfillment, this book will help you find your own successful comeback career. We want the stories of the women in this book to inspire you to rewrite yours.

Let's call BS on "invisible" once and for all.

It's your time to be fierce—this time for you. Get ready to begin your comeback career. You have value too.

1.

RESTLESS AND
READY TO REVOLT

Today's Midlife Career Crisis Is Real

Experienced, accomplished, and skilled professional forty-five-plus woman seeks to reinvent/return to a fulfilling career and paycheck. No problem, right?

—————

ONCE AGAIN, IT'S SEVEN O'CLOCK on that cold morning in December 2016, but three hundred miles south of the *Morning Joe* New York studio. My sister-in-law Ginny is alone in her home in Northern Virginia. Her teenagers, Will and Sophie, have just left for school and won't be back until dinnertime. Her husband, my brother Ian, left for work at 6:30 A.M. Ginny's a realtor, and a day of showing houses to potential clients looms ahead.

She's not looking forward to it.

Ginny and I have known each other since 1998, when she and my brother Ian started dating. Ginny worked on Capitol Hill, and I worked as a reporter for a TV station in Hartford, Connecticut. She chose a different career and life path from my own. After thirteen years in politics and policy, she off-ramped for a few years when her children were young. When they hit school age, she began what would become an eight-year career working in residential real estate. For that time in her life, real estate was the perfect fit.

Now her "mom duties" are waning—no more chauffeuring kids to games and doctors' appointments. Her schedule is about to be wide open, which, depending on her mood and hormone levels, can either make her cry (the kids are gone!) or ecstatic (the kids are gone!). With both kids about to be in college, she now has the opportunity to devote herself to a new career or passion or project—or all of the above. Real estate, her business for nearly the past decade, was the perfect work when the kids were younger, but it had always left her wanting more. She figures she's got two decades of work ahead, and she wants to make them count.

Just one problem: she has no idea how to begin. After all, who changes careers in her fifties?

It is all at once thrilling and overwhelming and scary.

What should she do? What can she do? How can she get there from here? The past near decade she's spent in real estate, but now she wants to make a sharp turn into something different. She'd had a top press secretary job on Capitol Hill, but that was back in the days of the fax machine. Her most recent experience, real estate, added negotiating, marketing, and a fair amount of real estate expertise to her bag of tricks. But the zigs and zags left her completely confounded, trying to figure out her next chapter. Where would she fit in today? What does she bring to the table in an organization? What industries or jobs might be adjacent to her previous work? Where would she need to upskill? How could she identify what industry or company or organization she should target? How could she convince a company or an organization that she could be an asset? Or, if she wanted to start her own business or something with friends, what would that look like?

And how do you begin all over again at the age of—gasp!—fifty-something? She'd had plenty of friends who'd paused and zigged and zagged, started new businesses, returned to work, or changed careers. Many were clearly crushing it—careers in high gear or embracing new paths and diving into entrepreneurial ventures or non-profits or even raising chickens. These weren't necessarily people who had stayed on the same career path, always leaning in, and now they, even after pausing, were hitting new heights.

Clearly, it could be done.

And fifty-(anything) is not what it used to be. Women—and men—are now rocking fifty. And sixty. And seventy. And seventy-nine (hello, Speaker Pelosi!).

Ginny was determined to move from the category of stuck and frustrated to leaping out of bed every morning and crushing it—she just needed to figure out how. She didn't need to be a CEO (yet); she just wanted a steady paycheck and meaningful work. She was tired of simply steering into the skid of a job that was no longer filling her tank, and now she had the time and bandwidth to do it. She knew she could add value somewhere. She just needed to find the right place and convince the right person. She needed a game plan—stat.

And that's when she texted me that December morning.

———

As we began researching this book, Ginny and I spoke with scores of women who were starting over, either by choice or by force. We heard inspiring, exasperating, courageous stories of women who had made the break with their lifelong career trajectory and set an entirely new course. Their individual circumstances may have been unique, but they shared common challenges. Despite some unexpected turns and early failures, the ones who were most successful had been proactive, strategic, and optimistic; they were able to shift toward something they wanted to do, not just needed to do. Most of them landed in a place that was better than where they were before in many ways—they truly felt they had made a comeback. They were back in control over their careers—and their lives.

These women fell into three general categories.

The Reinventers

Like Ginny, many women we spoke to felt a strong and growing urge for a career change. Some felt job-vulnerable, some were bored out of their minds, some yearned to finally do something with meaning. But the majority were experienced, accomplished, and skilled professional women hitting midlife and suddenly realizing they needed to make a career adjustment immediately.

"Sometimes I sit in these endless meetings, and I just think: *I cannot possibly do this for the next couple of decades. This job is not me anymore*," a fifty-something in banking told us.

Researchers say there's a U-shaped happiness curve in life that hits its nadir sometime in one's late forties or early fifties. The studies show that it is universal, regardless of socioeconomics. They say even chimps' and orangutans' happiness seems to plummet at their midlife, then head back up. This means that, if it's really a thing, maybe this midlife anxiety is biological, not societal. U curve or not, for many, the forties and fifties are a time of transitions and recalibration.

There's a parallel curve in work, say economists who have found that job satisfaction deteriorates at midlife. Former NPR journalist

Barbara Bradley Hagerty wrote in the *Atlantic* that only one-third of Gen X and Baby Boomer workers like their jobs, and 20 percent are "actively disengaged" or hate what they are doing.

Some of us are just profoundly burned out after decades of climbing the corporate ladder. Still others just feel a great restlessness and sense it's time to do something different. For Julianna Richter, former COO of PR at marketing consultancy firm Edelman, the realization that it was time to make a change came on slowly, as did the transition that followed. After several years at the same company, she had successfully worked her way up through five different high-level jobs. But then, in her late forties, with one child in college, she realized that although she loved her company, it was time, in her words, for a "conscious uncoupling" with her long-term work relationship.

"I didn't know what it was for a long time. I knew I wasn't happy, but I wasn't unhappy either," she told us. "I wasn't sitting there crying or hating my job. I was just restless. When the discussion of taking on a new role came up—which was very common at my company: every couple of years we'd be encouraged to move into a different role—instead of eliciting excitement the way it had in the past, I was resistant. That was the moment when I began to realize: I need a real change. The thing that had been bubbling up inside me that I couldn't even name. All of a sudden I was faced with a decision: Do I take a different role at the same company where I was comfortable, or do I leave? That was when I said, 'No, I think I need to break up.'"

After coming to this realization, Richter told her employer she wanted to "consciously uncouple," and over the next several months she transitioned out of her leadership position. She went through various "stages of grief" as she said goodbye to the company she helped grow, to her long-term colleagues (many who had become friends), and to the person she'd been for the last two decades. She worried about maintaining important relationships, and at times she struggled with doubts about her decision, but the more she talked about the transition, the more support she received from women wrestling with their own desire for change. Richter wrote on LinkedIn and Medium about the process of deliberately "uncoupling" from a long-term work relationship, and her piece went viral, with more than twenty thousand views. She was shocked by the number of women who reached out to tell her they were feeling the same thing and wanted to know exactly how she made the break. Clearly, she had hit a nerve.

Others reach midlife and sense their window of opportunity to do something they truly love is starting to close. "We were going through a difficult fundraise. If we didn't get this fund raised, I would have had to figure out what I would do next," a successful venture-capital partner told us. "I started thinking about that. I have a lot of different interests—sports, theater. I just started thinking, *What would I do?* We got through the fundraiser. But I kept thinking about it." She found herself searching for a new path, one with more meaning and creative expression. "I realized that every time I read about someone who had a really cool job or was doing something that I admired, they had risked something. And maybe at this age I really needed to reassess my relationship with risk."

Your definition of who you are—and who you should be—can be a sticking point for women at midlife. Consider: When you've been the same person for twenty-five-plus years, are you self-actualized, or are you just stuck in a routine? After an exhaustive job search, the venture-capital partner just couldn't find the right fit. "Then a woman friend of mine who had gone out on her own at the age of forty-nine said, 'Why don't you just do something on your own?' And I thought, *Why was I taking this option off the table?* You're increasingly hearing that women have to create the job they want because there are none out there." Now she's starting a lifestyle business for women forty-five and older.

All of these women hear the drumbeat of change and the voice inside that says, "It's time to move on." They're thinking about trying something different in their field or even an entirely different career, but starting over at midlife is daunting. But then the inner voice says, "If not now, when?"

The Returners

Then there are those who have taken a career break, either to raise children, care for aging relatives, or for myriad other reasons.

Anywhere from 2.4 to 3 million women have taken a career break and want to return to work. Many have advanced degrees and a decade or more of serious professional experience. They've been out of the workforce for one year—or maybe twenty. Now, by choice or necessity, it's time to get back to work. They are an untapped pool of talent, says Carol Fishman Cohen, who coined the term *relaunchers* for this group; in 2007 cowrote the original guide on returning to work, *Back on the Career Track*; and now helms iRelaunch, the global, seventy-five-thousand-member-strong, leading organization in returning to work after a career break. "High performers don't stop being high performers just because they took a career break," says Cohen. But it's tough to return after time away. Many find that the industry they left has changed profoundly or that their résumé gap prevents them from even getting an interview. And for many, technology has shifted how work is done and the skills that are required.

Caroline, now the associate general counsel at a top university, had been a practicing attorney at a big law firm before taking a sixteen-year break to raise her three sons. A few years ago she returned to the workforce via a midcareer re-entry program, and she quickly realized that the world of work had changed enormously. "Phones don't ring, and everyone does their own work—there are no secretaries. When I left the law firm where I worked, I didn't have a computer. I hand wrote my work, marked up a document, and handed it to somebody, and it was handed back to me. That's not how it is anymore. I skipped a huge turnaround in the workplace. It was a culture shock."

While she was away, not only had workflow systems evolved, but so did the way colleagues interact. Caroline had to get used to the fact that colleagues sitting right next to her would now email a question instead of speaking to her, that her boss was a full generation younger, and that she was expected to participate in colleagues' social media lives. The office culture she knew no longer existed.

Returners have to figure out their value and where their experience fits into this new landscape. They have to quickly upgrade their tech skills, stay open to things they don't know about, and find commonality in an intergenerational workspace. Whether they're looking to return to the same industry or trying to engage in a whole new career or entrepreneurial venture, they're facing a steep learning curve.

My best friend, Laura Eakin Erlacher, is a returner. Laura took a thirteen-year career break to raise her daughter, Eliza, and spent a very long time struggling to get back. Her story has a happy ending—she recently took a job as director of US Government Affairs and Policy for GE Power. We learned so much from her journey. I learned just how gritty and resilient my best friend is and that returning is absolutely possible—if you don't give up. And now we can't stop laughing about the fact that I'm about to take a summer vacation, and she's never going to see the light of summer again. (Sorry, Laura!) More on Laura's story later.

The Fired-at-Fifty Women

And then there are those who have been edged out of the work-force—and not by choice. These women don't have to work up the courage to leave a job—their employers cut the cord for them. For women at fifty and beyond who have been laid off or "restructured" or sense their job is tenuous: it's time to reinvent as soon as possible.

A joint Urban Institute–Pro Publica 2018 analysis of a health and retirement study found that a majority of adults in their *early fifties* are being pushed out of their jobs. Research shows that it is more difficult for women than it is for men to get back in. And only one in ten of them ever again earns as much as they had been making. Let that sink in.

"I was making too much money. They fired me and hired two people for my salary. With half my experience," reports one Fired at Fifty. Another told us that she's the oldest on her team, and she feels like she's got a target on her back. "I can't just wait. I need a backup plan," she told us.

The attrition rate for women in their fifties is nerve wracking. One lawyer we spoke to had returned to work at fifty-two. She thought she'd return to a group of her peers, but she was surprised to find that most of her colleagues were younger. She says the absence of women her age was bewildering. "I thought, *Where is everybody?* They weren't there. I now keep a little notebook of the over-fifty gals who leave—we're a shrinking group. I've been here for four years, and I keep wondering, *Where is everybody going?* To this day it really surprises me."

A 2018 survey by AARP found that one out of three workers felt their job was vulnerable due to their age. "There's something hay-wire about how women are expected to crunch our most celebrated achievements into a timetable that frequently lasts fewer than twenty years," says author and former *McCalls* editor-in-chief Sally Koslow in a viral *New York Times* column called "Hire Women Your Mom's Age." She broke down our expected timetable: "Find a partner. Raise some chicks. Zoom to the top of your field. Check each box by fifty."

What Is Up with Ageism and Women?

Age discrimination happens for all, but studies show—and we all know deep down—that women get hit harder than men. Certain industries are worse than others, of course—advertising, media . . . anything with an emphasis on youth or glamour. Television, as I will attest, can be brutal.

And of course technology has disrupted industries across the board and forced increasing numbers of midlife women to rethink their options. Lesley Jane Seymour, former editor-in-chief of *More*, *Marie Claire*, and *Redbook*, is a two-time reinventer and the founder of CoveyClub, an online and offline community for women who are forty-plus. She offered this observation: "When I went into publishing, a lot of people spent their entire careers at one magazine. If you had told me in my twenties that magazines would be a thing of the past by the time I was in my fifties, I would have laughed in your face. In a bazillion years nobody would have guessed."

When I told my friend Tina Brown, former editor-in-chief of *Vanity Fair* and the *New Yorker*, that we were writing this book, she recounted a story of a friend in her fifties who lost her job after being at the top of the magazine industry. "Women are told they cannot be employed at fifty-five. It is brutal."

According to the *Harvard Business Review*, the tsunami of corporate restructurings is expected to continue at an equal or faster pace in the next few years in response to market changes, leaving ever more pink-slipped job destruction in its wake.

My friend Liz Bentley is a leadership coach to top companies and talent. She says that in many cases men seem to have protections that women don't have. "I go into companies, and there are men who are in their eighties and still on the payroll making some money, whether they are adding value or not, and the same company is firing women at fifty because they are not relevant anymore. I've been in plenty of companies where the attitude is 'Y'know, he's not effective anymore, but he's Jim.' If Jim's name was Sally, she wouldn't be there. The second she wasn't effective, she would have been tossed. So while we do see the world changing, many men have incredible protection when it comes to income that women don't have."

Yikes.

Ageism—and, particularly, gendered ageism—may be illegal, but it is hard to prove and, unfortunately, a fact of life. Not only are older workers more vulnerable to job loss in the first place, but employers are also reluctant to hire older workers because they consider their salaries too expensive or believe they will cost more in health benefits. Employers also worry about the cost of training older workers and not being able to recoup those costs because they assume those workers won't stay as long as they near retirement age. And then there's the perception that workers in their fifties and beyond are just slow and tech troglodytes. Why hire someone who might be a drain on resources when you can hire younger workers (aka "digital natives") for less money?

Looking for a job when you're over fifty and female can feel like a liability. I laughed at Ginny when she told me she took her birth year off her Facebook page and her graduation year off her résumé. It wasn't vanity, she told me; it was an act of economic self-preservation. In a 2019 survey Know Your Value conducted with NBC we asked women if they felt compelled to lie about their age or maybe just fudge it a little either at work or during job searches. We found that 20 percent of them felt they needed to conceal their age. And it's not just us: a 2019 AP-NORC Center poll found that nearly eight in ten women aged fifty and older feel that their age is a hindrance when job seeking. For men, that number is 70 percent.

And yet older workers are a growing part of the workforce. Since 2005 older workers—defined by the US Bureau of Labor Statistics as fifty-five and older—have made up a larger share of the labor force than those aged sixteen to twenty-four. For most of them, early retirement just isn't an option. According to that same AP-NORC Center poll, nearly half of American adults expect—because they want or need—to work beyond sixty-five. In 1995 that number was only 14 percent. Yet too many are shown the door before they are ready to leave. An Urban Institute analysis showed that the number of "forced retirements" for the sixty-five-and-up age group has increased from 33 percent in 1998 to 55 percent in 2014, while over that same time period satisfaction with "retirement" has dropped. In other words, most women (and men) today don't want and/or can't afford to retire at sixty-something.

The longer we want to work, the more we are likely to run into age bias—especially women. That needs to change.

It's Time to Stage Your Comeback

Let's change the narrative and reimagine the possibilities of mid- to late-career reinvention. We want to find new opportunities and new context in a world of work that doesn't have a roadmap for women who want or need to work beyond the traditional retirement age. We want to make changes that will help us work better, longer.

We need to create our own comebacks, because the fact is that our numbers are growing: older women are playing a much bigger role in today's labor force. According to the Bureau of Labor Statistics, women over fifty-five are the fastest growing age/gender workforce category—3.6 million women over fifty-five will be added to the US workforce by 2026. In contrast, the number of men over fifty-five working is projected to decline by 3 percent.

I'd like to think about midlife as a time to assess and adjust. "Fifty really is halftime," my friend Stephanie Carter said when I told her I was writing this book. "Why do you have this ritual of half time? To think about how you played the first half and apply that to your second half." Stephanie is reinventing after a successful career in venture capital. She's starting a media company for women our age who she thinks are, in a way, pioneers. "In every vein of our lives, health and wellness, investments, we are seeing that long-held assumptions [about how to structure the second half of our lives] are probably not true, and we're the first generation that can recognize and make active choices around that." Leadership coach Liz Bentley agrees: "The thirties are when you are having your babies, the forties are when you are raising your babies, and the fifties through seventies can be your greatest earning years." So let's start making those active choices and take control of the rest of our working lives—now.

A big part of this is mindset—you're pushing back against a long-standing ageist narrative and blazing a new trail, so restarting or reinventing your career at midlife may require an attitude adjustment not just by society but within yourself as well. As we were working on this book, Ginny reached out to her Facebook community and asked them what they thought about this time in our lives. How did they feel about "midlife"? She got a huge response—from both women and men. Some said they could care less, that midlife is just a fact—this age (forty-five to fifty) is midlife (if we're lucky!). Some agreed that the word *midlife* has negative connotations, mainly because of its association with the word "crisis," but that they felt positively about this time of life. Some suggested new terms: halftime, intermission, the wise years, experienced, midcareer, middle age, primetime.

They defined this time as "the assessment years." They felt self-actualized and "adult" in a way that younger people either aren't or don't consider themselves to be. Others argued that midlife suggests potential because "if you're only halfway through your life, think what opportunities and adventures lie ahead." Nobody wanted to call it a "crisis"—as one friend said, these are the "Best badass years of your life. All the wisdom with the body and mind to use it!"

CoveyClub's Seymour agrees, saying that the young don't hold the monopoly on "having potential." "I believe we have enormous potential—plus the knowledge and savvy and perhaps, finally, the funds—to reinvent ourselves. We have the potential to go back to school to pursue new adult dreams. We have the potential to change direction to rethink our relationships with our mates, with our homes, with our communities. We have great potential to contribute in a new way to the corporations we work for or to the world around us. We have the potential to transform from great parents into great coaches and friends for our kids. Potential is a mindset. . . . Midlife is the time you get to reset your clock, reset your needs and your wishes, to give the finger to what society says . . . about everything. This is your time."

Yes.

It will take all of us to change minds about ageism in the workplace. Women need to speak up about the issue and help combat it by hiring older women. It's up to us to make ourselves visible and relevant. And not just for us—it's for today's thirty-something women too. As Sally Koslow observes, "Today's thirty- and forty-somethings can't 'lean in' forever. If they don't address embedded ageism, they'll blink, pass fifty, and possibly see their success evaporate faster than a boss can say, 'Sorry, we're going in another direction'—a younger direction."

Together, by our intention and our example, we will change the face of work. As more of us work, achieve, and succeed well into our fifties, sixties, and even seventies, we will change attitudes. I know I plan to keep working for decades. My eighty-eight-year-old mother is still wielding her chainsaw, creating soaring sculptures out of massive logs. I have tried to get her to slow down—after all, it's a chainsaw! But work—in her case, art—is where she gets her superpowers.

Ginny and I wanted to know: How do some women get the courage to reinvent a career when all the signs around them seem to say, "It can't be done," "It's too risky," "You're past your prime," "You're doomed to fail"? How do you say, "Yes, I can—and I will." What is the difference between someone who feels paralyzed by an adverse job situation and someone who turns a bad situation into an opportunity? What is the impetus deep inside that turns them from being crushed to crushing it? How do we tap into our power? What is the key to getting unstuck?

And how do I get some of that?

2.

GET YOUR
CONFIDENCE ON

Let's go back in time a few years for a story about me. It was 2004, and I had finally made it in broadcast news. After years of dues paying, I was in line for my first big-time network contract. I'd been working at CBS as a correspondent and occasional fill-in anchor and was in line to be a regular *Sunday News* anchor and correspondent for *60 Minutes Wednesday*. In my new role I would also contribute to *CBS Sunday Morning* and the *Evening News*—it was everything I wanted at that stage of my career. Then a series of events changed everything: Dan Rather was fired, *60 Minutes Wednesday* was canceled, CBS management changed, and Katie Couric was hired to anchor weeknights. And, just like that, CBS no longer needed me. With the words, "It's not going to work out," I was fired on my thirty-ninth birthday. I'd done nothing wrong. I'd even made it clear that I was willing to renegotiate my contract and work for less because my responsibilities had changed with the cancellation of *60 Minutes Wednesday*. When I asked why I was being let go, I was told simply that the decision was "subjective." What did that even mean? It was bad enough being fired, but the lack of clarity haunted me for a long, long time.

My year-long involuntary career break was an awful time. I really despaired that I'd never work again. When I wasn't freaking out about money, I wondered how I would fill my days. My career had defined my identity in so many ways, and without it I felt lost. I missed the adrenaline rush, the camaraderie of my colleagues, and the work itself. My job search was a disaster.

Months went by, and I decided I'd better widen my search. I applied for a few jobs in public relations, which I knew I could handle. I had the skill set, even if my heart would not be in it. Ironically, my PR interviews were excellent, but when a perfectly good PR job was offered to me, I got cold feet. Instead, I encouraged the firm to hire a friend whom I knew would be a better fit. I literally gave away a senior-level job with predictable hours at an excellent firm and would have paid $300,000. But I knew that I would have been miserable and, as a result, probably fail. I had to walk away.

I thought I had it in me to start something entirely new—but I didn't. Not then.

Even with no prospects in sight, I realized I just wasn't ready to give up on television news. That was where my heart was, even if no one else seemed to think I belonged there. I begged my agent to send me out on more interviews—and to include lower-level positions. This time, I promised, I really knew that I wanted to be at MSNBC. I was willing to take virtually any job there to get back in. I had worked there for two years, knew the culture, and was sure that if I could just get my foot in the door with a little on-air job, the team I loved would put me to more productive use, and I would flourish.

On this last desperate call to MSNBC, my agent's associate managed to get a nibble. A crazy, entry-level nibble. There was a part-time job doing cut-ins at a day rate on an on-call basis. The team at MSNBC was shocked I would even consider it. I was most definitely, hugely, incredibly overqualified. This job was entry-level broadcast journalism—and freelance, at that! A year ago I'd been a comfortably salaried, queen-bee, network anchor. Even my previous job at MSNBC eight years earlier on the weekday afternoon show *Homepage*, when about three people watched MSNBC, had been much more senior. And the money was a joke. But I didn't even need to give it thirty seconds of thought: I took it. No cold feet and no regrets.

As soon as I accepted it, I felt better, like an instantaneous reboot. I was back to work. I was rebuilding my confidence. I was excited to get up every morning. And the "just getting a foot in the door" thing and starting at the bottom again? It worked. I knew what I was doing—I could have done those cut-ins in my sleep. Nonetheless, I worked my tail off and said yes to every assignment, including the news cut-ins on a little show called *Scarborough Country* . . . and the rest is history.

The funny thing is that if you had said to me when I was thirty-nine, "Ten years from now you're gonna get fired. How are you going to feel?" I would have said to myself, *Well, that's basically it. I'm never getting back in.* But what I've learned between thirty-nine and forty-nine—about my value in the marketplace and my personal values—has made me so much stronger. I'm so much more comfortable with myself than I was at thirty-nine. I know why I didn't get hired for a long time—because I walked in there questioning every word that came out of my mouth. I was so horrified by that failure, so horrified by that embarrassment, so horrified by the loss of my identity that I literally could not pull together a reasonable pitch about who I was. But now, in my fifties, just try me.

Now when some doors close, I know there are others I can open. All of a sudden, at this age, closed doors are not so frightening. I'm ready for anything now, much more ready than I was at thirty-nine with two little kids.

Where does this confidence come from? For me, it comes from having survived a lot of hard knocks. I put up daily with so much nonsense on social media. I've been bullied by the president. (Really, at this point, who hasn't?) My job is on the line every day. And all of this has made me stronger and more confident.

When we talk about women pulling the trigger on major life change, we always come back to the issue of confidence. Half of my time at my Know Your Value conferences is spent focusing on confidence—having the confidence necessary to ask for a promotion or a raise and to speak up in meetings. Lack of confidence is the thread that runs through so many challenges that women face—especially women who are starting a new career after being in a different field or out of the workforce altogether.

Confidence is a critical component of success in anything. Confidence gets you off the couch, lets you make that phone call, pushes you to introduce yourself at a networking event, and gets you out from behind your laptop when you are looking for a job. It's the ability to just believe you can do something—to quell the voices in your head that say you can't or shouldn't.

Why do women in particular seem to struggle with confidence? My good friends, BBC anchor and *Morning Joe* colleague Katty Kay and ABC News's Claire Shipman, explore this perceived confidence deficit in their best-seller, *The Confidence Code*. They interviewed neuroscientists, met with a variety of women leaders, and pulled from their own personal experience. Ultimately, they found that there is indeed an acute confidence gap that separates the sexes, and it's partly biological and partly social. But you don't have to accept that reality. You can actively cultivate self-confidence by trying, failing, surviving, acknowledging your resilience, and, ultimately, succeeding. And when action leads to success? As Katty likes to say, "Confidence occurs when the insidious self-perception that you aren't able is trumped by the stark reality of your achievements."

The Value of Life Experience

So let's look at reality. What do women at midlife have going for them that younger women don't? How can they feel confident about their true value in the workplace?

What do midlife and older women really bring to the table?

If you're in your late forties, fifties, or beyond, you have broad experience and "historic wins." A woman of this age simply has had more time than her younger counterparts to accumulate accomplishments and practical knowledge. You have what Liz Bentley calls "historic wins"—the times in your life that you believe you succeeded and had a win. "These wins can vary from big things like a hard-to-get promotion to smaller wins like giving a presentation," says Bentley. "These wins often display your strengths, resilience, and ability to succeed." Bentley says when you are looking to make a comeback in your career, revisiting historical wins helps you build a foundation of confidence. Some people are very connected to their historical wins and can rattle them off rapid-fire. These people know their strengths and look to those wins to build more confidence for their future career. Bentley says that for others it may not be quite as obvious and that they need to think harder to find them, perhaps because their wins aren't as tangible. Bentley cites an example: "I have a client who is great at collaborating. She can get along with any personality, but she didn't see that as a strength. However, it is a huge strength, especially in business, where your ability to get along with all types of people, navigate difficult personalities, and bring everyone together to collaborate is incredibly valued. Once we identified this as a strength, she realized that she had tons of historic wins using it." So dig deep to remember your wins and tell yourself: *I believe in myself and I can do this—I have had wins before. I will have wins again.*

You have pattern recognition. You've been there, done that, seen it, and know how to handle it. With age comes a much wider frame of reference of both personal and professional experience, which translates to better judgement. As one midlife empty-nester pointed out, "For us, at this stage we've lived a good chunk of life, and the benefit is that our practical knowledge is extensive. It's huge. We're like Siri, but with heart."

You have self-knowledge. By the time you're in your forties and fifties, you know yourself. You know where you excel and where you don't. (And if you still need help on that, read on!) You know what makes you better than someone else at a particular job. As former senator Claire McCaskill says, "Once you own what you're good at, then the only other step that's left is for you to market yourself." In other words, once you know your value, all you have to do is articulate it.

You are old enough to know your power, and I am here to tell you that age does not diminish it. Here's an excellent example: Speaker of the House Nancy Pelosi first ran for Congress at age forty-seven, when the youngest of her five children was a senior in high school. In 2001 she was elected House minority whip, then minority leader in 2002. In 2007, at the age of sixty-six, she became the first female Speaker of the House. In 2019 she was elected Speaker again. That's a comeback career! When I asked Speaker Pelosi the difference between Nancy Pelosi now and who she was thirty years ago, she said she would always speak her mind, only now she would speak with confidence, not just brashness. She has confidence that only experience can bring. I talk a lot about knowing your value—she calls it "knowing your power."

You have broader, wider, and more powerful networks than you did a few decades ago. Whether you've been working or on a career break, at this age you simply know more people and have more connections. And you're now savvy enough to know how to use those networks. The investments you have made in relationships, groups, and communities over the decades will pay off.

You have the sisterhood. Maybe it's a side effect of #MeToo, but it seems that women our age are collaborating more and competing less with each other. We know that having each other's backs is how we are going to fight and win against sexism and gendered ageism.

You've got business skills. Women who have been in the workforce for two or three decades have learned a thing or two. They can manage multiple projects, set priorities, and meet deadlines. They not only know how to do their job; they are also strong communicators and collaborators—they know how to function effectively as colleagues.

You grew up having real conversations with real people—not texting or Snapchatting as a substitute for all verbal communication. You've mastered the lost art of In Real Life. You are highly prized for your ability to talk to people instead of staring at your phone. Call me old fashioned, but this, girlfriends, is an asset you've got over the twenty-something set.

Even if you have been out of the paid workforce for a while or are launching into a completely different field, you still have vital "soft" skills. "A lot of core team skills never go out of style—managing others, being able to resolve conflict, having effective sales negotiation and communication skills," says Alexandra Cavoulacos of TheMuse.com. "Many of those core soft skills are more valued than ever and highly transferable. Those are the things that are going to be harder for computers and AI to supplant."

And if you've been an at-home parent? Lean into it. MSNBC's Stephanie Ruhle says stay-at-home moms can't discount the proficiencies they've developed over the course of everyday life: "What do you think a PTA president does? What do you think a class mom does? [They're] organizing and executing." That's a critical skill set to have. Moms know how to get things done—because they don't have another option. They've learned how to multitask and work efficiently, and if they don't know how to do something, they figure it out. We talked to a number of women who returned to work or started new businesses after years of caring for their special-needs children. These women had successfully navigated massive healthcare and educational bureaucracies. They could teach a master class in persistence, personal advocacy, bookkeeping, and maneuvering complex systems fraught with arcane regulations and human error. They have skills and chutzpah to spare.

If you are about to be an empty-nester, you have more time, are less conflicted, are more stable, are through with maternity leaves, and are probably almost finished with carpooling. Your schedule is clearing, it is your turn, and you are ready for takeoff. You can give an employer 110 percent, or you can start your own business and give it 110 percent. You can lead a movement, run for office, start a nonprofit, change the world. You've got the bandwidth and a long runway, and you are ready to have an impact and live your truth.

Through your paid and unpaid work, you've proven you have a strong work ethic. You are mature and responsible, and you finish the job because you're a grown-up. Take it from legendary broadcast journalist and TV host Meredith Viera, who has pivoted to different roles throughout her career. I asked her what the sixty-year-old Meredith brings to a job that the thirty-year-old Meredith did not, and she told me, "The sixty-year-old Meredith brings a much stronger skill set, can handle crisis with calm, and has a sense of humor about myself. I take my work seriously but not myself seriously." Most of all, she says, she's driven to work hard and can bring all of her experience to bear on each new project. "I have a strong desire to work—I have a very strong desire to be there, and I know I can make things better because of my age and skills."

By the time you reach midlife, you've also learned resilience. Think about it: you too have taken risks, recovered from failure, weathered your share of disappointments, and survived on-the-job disasters. You are literally time tested. You may have more failures in your past than someone in their twenties, but you've also earned more victories and gained the strength that comes from picking yourself up and trying again. "If necessary, write [your experiences] down on a list," says Katty Kay. "Write them all down, literally as a reminder: *here are the things that I have achieved in my life*. It's amazing what that can do to just bring that needle back in line with reality."

With maturity you probably care less about what people think. When I passed the age of fifty I suddenly felt a freedom—a lack of caring about what other people think—but not in a bad way. In a brave way. I was actually confused by how great I felt about myself as I became more mature. I think, like so many women, I had been carrying a lot of baggage, a lot of worry about what other people thought, and to age out of that was disorienting.

So next time you default to feeling bad about your age (or neck, as the late, great Erma Bombeck said), just stop. *Seriously. Stop.* Go back and read this list—which, by the way, is just a drop in the bucket of how great you are *right now*. I am deeply tired of hearing the word *invisible*. Stop worrying about what "they" are thinking, because the reality is that they're not thinking anything (come on, they are so busy Snapchatting on their phones—they are clueless!). *You* are stronger, wiser, and better, and it is time you recognized and acted on that. Take back your power, and own these decades. Start raising your hand and putting yourself out there to win. Flick off failure. Start saying yes. Discover and fuel your purpose. You will never get an opportunity unless you go out and grab it. So show your value and make the world a better place—because you *can*.

3.

BUT FIRST . . . GET OUT OF YOUR OWN WAY

Stronger, wiser, better—that's what we are in our forties, fifties, and beyond. Life experience may be a formidable advantage, but we tend to forget just how powerful we are and how fierce we can be. So many of us face roadblocks of our own devising. So here's the tough-love section, with help again from my friend and leadership coach Liz Bentley.

An executive coach and president of Liz Bentley Associates, Bentley works with me on the Know Your Value conferences, has coached my Grow Your Value contestants, and has worked with women who want to transition back to work. She says the challenges facing midlife women in a career transition are as much internal as external challenges, like getting your résumé or LinkedIn profile up to speed. We talked to Bentley for her advice about dealing with psychological barriers for career returners and reinventers.

"What I see as the biggest hurdle in making a change is facing and understanding your inner journey," Bentley told us. "This is the journey where you see your truth, work through obstacles, let go of excuses, find courage to be different, stare down your fears, and evolve and grow into the best version of yourself. People often don't make [a] change because it is hard, and they create roadblocks for themselves."

Personally, I think we need to be willing to learn from our mistakes—I've certainly done so in my own life. In order to grow, we need to be open to evolving. For women in midlife, especially those trying to break back into the work world, establishing yourself in a new position or a new career can feel like learning a brand-new language. Some women are impatient to get their value back right away, but many times we have to rebuild from the ground up, and that can be a vulnerable experience. When things don't go exactly as we hope or if an interaction doesn't go well, it's easy to overreact. It's easy to start putting up barriers so you feel protected from your own fears. You start to see every bump in the road as a sign and tell yourself things like, *Well, maybe I'm not ready to go back, or maybe this isn't something I really want to do.* When you research a certain job or business idea, you start to notice only the negative aspects or the potential disaster ahead because you're just not completely ready to dive back in. You need to be mentally ready to learn all over again and to find the strength to pick yourself up after the inevitable complications and disappointments.

So how do we deal with these barriers—the inner hurdles, the mental blocks, and the limiting beliefs?

See and Understand Your Truth. "People need to be able to see their truth in order to evolve," says Bentley. "If you don't see your truth, you don't know where you are on the map. You don't really know your geography, which makes it hard to plot your course. Seeing your truth is powerful, but it can feel painful. We don't even know where to start if we don't know where we are standing." It's about being self-aware, getting a realistic idea of what our value is at this moment, not what we project it to be in the future or from the past. Bentley says we do this by listening to feedback, both formal (e.g., you ask a colleague for feedback on your résumé) and informal (e.g., you are not getting any callbacks), and being open to different perspectives of your truth. We get informal feedback all the time, and we want to pay attention to it because it gives us valuable insights into ourselves as well as a reality check. Feedback is one way of understanding your truth—your current place on the map. Don't be afraid of seeing your truth. "What I find is that sometimes, if people are starting to get stuck, it's because they're really struggling with seeing that truth. They get afraid of seeing it—it's like a monster in a closet."

Here's an example: Maybe you've been a stay-at-home mom for a couple of years. You have a law degree, you used to be at a law firm, and you're ready to go back to work as an attorney, so you start getting your résumé out there, but no one is responding. So your truth may be that you might need to start at a lower position than you were hoping for. Your place on the map isn't where you thought it was, and you need to adjust. Or sometimes your truth can be that an experience you had is extremely valuable on your résumé—something you may not have thought was a big deal. But a different perspective on it may show your resilience, that you are quick on your feet, that you can solve problems. Getting different perspectives—some may be bad, some may be good—on your truth is important.

Solution: Be open to feedback, and get it from multiple sources, every step of the way—on your résumé, LinkedIn profile, and job targets. Listen for the informal feedback too—the calls that aren't getting returned, the emails that go unanswered. Fold it into your journey, acknowledge it, and try to make changes. Don't get mad or throw in the towel when you get negative feedback, rejections, or no call-backs; instead, adjust, recalibrate, and keep moving forward.

Let Go of Excuses. Another common impediment to women who are relaunching and reinventing: finding the time and urgency to act on their own behalf. A lot of women, when they're returning after raising kids or just trying to juggle job searching while caregiving, find that life keeps taking over. Sometimes it becomes an excuse: "I can't start on this big transition or look for a job because I have to help my kids/parents/spouse with XYZ." It's so easy to reflexively put everyone else first and let your own goals be secondary. But— hello! Recognize that this may be an artificial barrier that you are putting up. If you really want this, you need to make it a priority.

Sometimes we erect these roadblocks on purpose because it keeps us safe and confirms the false narrative that we can't go back or make a change. We say, "I can't miss a game," "I can't miss an outing," "I need to drive my kids to school," "I'm too old," "I've committed to this committee," "I'll start later." But if you really want to do this, you need to get rid of your roadblocks.

"I think a lot of women stop and get out of the doing because they get stuck in the thinking," says Bentley. "I run into women all the time who've been talking about going back to work for years or having false starts into things they don't follow through with. After a while it's enough talking—you have to start acting. I say to people all the time: How much longer would you like to be talking about this? How long have you been talking about going back to work or changing careers, and how much longer do you want to talk about it? In sales, you have to have a hundred lines in the water to get two bites. That means you have to make a hundred contacts, send a hundred emails. You have to do all these things, all the time, to get one person to bite. I'll see these women who will send one email and be like, 'I didn't get a response' instead of saying, 'I sent a hundred emails this week.' In the restart, you have to get out of the thinking and get into the doing because it's gonna take a lot of doing to get one thing to happen. It takes grit and resilience."

Are we going to be having this same conversation next year at this time? I hope not!

Returner Alicia Schober is a perfect example of how to do it. Alicia had been out for eighteen years, but on her fiftieth birthday the Cupertino, California, mom of two decided she was ready to get back to work. She spoke to us about the need to focus on yourself despite the distraction of family life. "It takes dedication to yourself. It takes saying, *I will do this.* For sixteen and a half months I worked three hours a day on my relaunch. I would tell my family that I am going to do my homework and don't want to be disturbed for a few hours. If you are working full time and are trying to figure out a pivot, you need to make that commitment to yourself. You need to come home and spend this time doing some introspection and scout sources to help. You need to *allow* yourself to do this."

It is your turn. "The 'make-it-happen attitude' is the trademark of many moms, and we use it regularly on behalf of our children," says author Melissa Shultz, who wrote *From Mom to Me Again* about preparing for and reinventing her life after her children left for college. "But when it comes to us, especially at this stage of life, we often forget how to be our own best cheering section."

Solution: Have a goal and hold yourself accountable. Make a timeline. What do you want to accomplish, and by when? Sure, you'll need to spend some time going through the discernment phase and figuring out what you want to do and putting together your résumé and LinkedIn profile, but don't let that prevent you from the action phase of making contacts and applying for jobs. When you have a timeline, you become accountable and recognize when you are holding yourself back with excuses. You can look back at your week and see if you got your emails and calls done . . . or if you were at the gym for ten hours. That spin class may be good for your quads, but it is not going to get you closer to your career goal.

We asked Bentley to break down a potential timeline for us: "Let's say it's July 2020, and you want a job by January 2021. In order for that to happen, you need to have traction and be in interviews by the fourth quarter of 2020. For that to happen, you have to get on people's radars. So during July and August you need to be cranking out emails and phone calls and doing a ton of meetings and seeing where you are getting traction. Remember: you need a hundred lines in the water for two bites. You need to be figuring out what is working and what is not working. You need to figure out where you are on the map—are you in Siberia, or are you in Iceland, closer to the mainland? Where are you if no one is responding? You are in Siberia. How do you get out of Siberia? The only one who is getting you out of Siberia is you. Your informal feedback was that nobody responded. Time to get formal feedback. Time to sit down with three people so you can have different versions of the truth so you can understand how to evolve. Bring your stuff—your résumé, cover letters, pitch, targeted jobs—and ask, 'What do you think of this?' 'How do I make it better?' Don't be afraid of difference."

Don't let others trigger you. This is a stressful process, and you are likely to be triggered. *Triggers* are the things people say that can send us into a tailspin. They are a poke at our subconscious that can shut us down emotionally. In that way, triggers are another form of roadblocks. Everyone has different triggers, Bentley tells us, but your *behavior* is in your control. "If someone or something triggers you, it's your issue, not theirs. You own your triggers, and even if the situation is affecting others as well, don't join the bandwagon. It's your responsibility to rise, regardless of the situation." Both Ginny and I had triggers when we were working on this book, and I think there are lessons to be learned from this. For example, even though we went into this project wanting to become closer, Ginny let me know about how she perceives me as someone who has a huge success story, while she is trying to figure out her own next steps. I had to let her know that I am as vulnerable and raw inside as she is about the decisions I have made and the place where I am in life. We worked hard, we dug deep, and we really worked through some incredible triggers. And the discussions helped us write a better book as well as understand ourselves on a much deeper level.

Know your triggers, and don't let them throw you from your mission.

Act More, Think Less. Nothing will happen unless you start. Women have a tendency to ruminate, especially after setbacks. Being fired from a job you love is soul crushing and can send you into a spiral of doing nothing but obsessing over the problem at hand. My year off after I was fired from CBS was brutal. I had a hard time sustaining motivation to look for a job when my self-worth was shot.

But there is deep value in taking action, even action that leads to failure. Failure can teach you what not to do and convince you that the world doesn't end even if things go wrong. It really does make you stronger and more confident.

My friend Jane Pauley learned the value of taking action after her daytime talk show was canceled in 2005. She admits she was at sea for a while considering the next step. She says she sunk into her living room sofa and stayed there for a good long time—thinking, looking, and ideating about what was next.

She was looking for something—but that "something" was ill defined.

This sounds shocking coming from the uber successful Jane Pauley. Jane's incredible career includes co-anchoring the *Today Show* from 1976 to 1989, cohosting *Dateline NBC* for more than a decade, helming her own daytime talk show, and now anchoring the top-rated, critically acclaimed *CBS Sunday Morning* as well as authoring several books.

However, after *The Jane Pauley Show* was canceled in 2005 after a single season, Jane says she got too comfortable on the couch thinking about what was next without actually doing something about it. As she tells it, she was too long on "think" and too short on "do."

"I just took for granted that was the end of my television career," Jane told us. "In TV you cease to exist. There I was: I was fifty-four, and it was over, and there was absolutely nothing for me.

"But deep down I knew my productive life was not over. I struggled for four years but finally found the answer. I was not looking for some whiz-bang second act. I just needed to feel productive, like there was meaning in my life. . . . I still felt like I was in my prime and didn't want to squander that opportunity."

Her son, then twenty-four, gave her a wise nudge. "In an email he said I'd spent enough time thinking and that it was time 'to make something happen.'"

And she did.

She took one of her ideas and reconnected with the *Today Show*. For four years she did monthly segments coproduced with AARP called "Your Life Calling." She later turned those stories into a book. That book got the attention of a producer at *CBS Sunday Morning*. An interview on the show about the book led to a job as a contributor to the broadcast in 2014. Then in 2016, at the age of sixty-four and nearly forty years to the day after she started on the *Today Show*, Jane became the anchor of *CBS Sunday Morning*.

"That was something I never imagined, and yet I made it happen," Jane says of anchoring *CBS Sunday Morning*.

"Sometimes—to kind of quote Rascal Flatts—it's that broken road that leads you straight to something," Jane says. "You've got to get on the road and just start anything. Stop making lists. Close the book. Just do something, and a year later who knows where that will lead."

Pauley reaffirms our own experiences—when I started over doing cut-ins at MSNBC and when Ginny said yes to writing for Know

Your Value. "Don't wait for the one, true, perfect thing," says Jane. "Just go and do something—anything. Say yes."

Just say yes.

Be Brave. For many women considering a reboot, there's the fear of failure or rejection, the fear of being out of the loop and rusty, the fear of being too old, the fear of embarrassing yourself. The fears may be overblown (age and rejection) and completely irrational (embarrassing yourself) or are things that you can actually do something about (get up to date and unrusty). Still, they can paralyze us. Bentley says we need to face our fears—and sometimes situations simply force us to deal with them.

That was the case with Ginny's friend Helen, who suddenly, at the age of fifty, found herself divorced and without an income after a twenty-year career break. Everything in her world was falling apart. Her marriage had just dissolved, her teenage twin daughters had developed serious health issues, and after two decades out of the workforce, she needed to find work—fast. She stopped calling many of her friends, who worried about her. It was, she says, just too much to explain everything that had gone wrong in her life.

Helen had been an expert in her field. After earning a master's degree in fine and decorative American art, Helen had worked at Sotheby's Auction House in New York, then spent time managing art galleries in the city before moving with her young children to Virginia, where she settled into a life of volunteer work and raising her children. A decade later her husband's work moved the family to Connecticut, and five years later she found herself divorced and looking for work. "There was so much fear in this process. Fear of failure, of not being up to it. My own fear that I would never find joy again," she says.

But serendipity intervened in the shared parking lot of a school and an auction house in a small town in Connecticut. "I had brought my daughter to visit a school and noticed that the school shared a parking lot with an auction house that I had never heard of. I sent the auction house my résumé, and two weeks later I was called in for an interview. They happened to be looking for someone with my qualifications. After twenty years I went back to exactly the same thing I was doing."

Her lesson learned? "The truth is that the fear is bigger than the reality."

Solution: Stop letting things make you cower. Instead, do something. If you are afraid of being rusty in tech, take an online class. Feeling old? Get inspired by reading about all the women and men who are crushing it at fifty-plus (WeAreAgeist.com) or listen to Lesley Jane Seymour's reinvention podcasts (CoveyClub.com). Afraid of failure or rejection? Bring it on. The best thing you can do is learn from it.

Take a Risk. Another roadblock women experience: a reluctance to venture beyond their comfort zone. They are pinned down by a lack of confidence. But the truth is that nothing builds confidence like taking action, especially when the action involves risk or even failure.

When I asked Ginny to speak at my Know Your Value conference in October of 2017, it was only the second time she had spoken in front of a large audience. The first time had been two weeks prior, at Carol Fishman Cohen's iRelaunch conference. She said she was in flight-or-fight mode for days leading up to each event. She had memorized answers to my questions . . . and then I asked her different questions. I had no idea how nervous she was—and she's my sister-in-law. But getting outside her comfort zone and accepting risk, although immensely uncomfortable for her, was ultimately a confidence builder.

"I was so relieved when it was over, but I also felt like if I could do that, then I could handle other things," says Ginny. Mika's "last-minute choice to ask unexpected questions may have fried my nerves, but I left the auditorium feeling stronger than ever." And she's now over her fear and doing a lot more public speaking.

Build your confidence by trying things outside your comfort zone.

Believe in yourself and they will too. Nobody needs to know the doubts running through your head. Bentley and I both believe that it is critically important to project confidence and strength . . . even if you have to fake it for a while. Energy, passion, and a positive attitude help too. If you believe in yourself, other people will too, whether it's on a job search or a project you are working on.

"It's all about what you project to people," says nonprofit executive Susan Thaxton. Thaxton had been out of the workforce for a few years and told us that she learned a key lesson about the power of projection when she attended Harvard Business School's Charting Your Path, a conference for women at a transitional point in their careers. The experience, she told us, was life changing.

"I went there with the idea that I've got to figure out how to define myself to fit in somebody else's box. I needed to know how can I define myself in their terms so that they'll hire me." She came away with the realization that she was already marketable. She already filled key boxes. She just had to believe in herself.

Her big *A-ha!* moment came when each conference participant was asked to review a list of one hundred job titles and circle the twenty they would want to do. Thaxton volunteered to go up to the chalkboard and choose her twenty careers in front of the audience, then list them in the order of her preference—in her case, COO, captain of a ship, running a resort . . .

Later that day participants had a chance to talk to each other and share advice. Thaxton was surprised to find three or four people in line waiting to talk to her. She was amazed that they all "wanted to talk to me because of what I had written on the board. I realized that they associated me with those titles just because I wrote them down and stood in front of them. . . . In their mind—that's who I was."

Thaxton learned an important lesson that day, one that wasn't on the Harvard agenda: "In my head I was a stay-at-home mom who does X. A stay-at-home mom who is trying to do consulting. A stay-at-home mom who is trying to go back to work." Her advice? Take the "stay-at-home mom" piece out of the equation when you are talking about your professional goals and aspirations. Talking about yourself in a different way makes all the difference.

My friend Meredith Viera echoes this sentiment when it comes to dealing with ageism. She told me that the challenge is to "develop faith in yourself and to project that faith and confidence. I am sixty-five, and I know that ageism is out there. I say a mantra. I literally say to myself, 'Yes, I am an older woman, but with that comes experience and maturity.' If you project what you want to, it will be reflected back at you."

Confidently project who and what you want to be—otherwise known as "fake it 'til you make it."

And for Pete's sake, stop apologizing. Own your story, and everyone else will too. So you have a zig-zag career history and/or you've got a résumé gap. You know what? That's probably not the problem. It might be your own lack of confidence that's selling you short. "You need to own it," Bentley tells us. "Once you own your story, everyone else will too. I worked as a ski instructor in Aspen for a year after college. When I went to interview for jobs, I didn't apologize or let them bully me into thinking it was a bad choice. I owned my decision and made it sound incredible, and it was. Your résumé reflects your life experiences and choices, so own them and be proud of what you picked and say, 'This is what I do, and this is how I am going to add value for you.'" Bentley took a look at Ginny's résumé and told her she needed to change her perspective. It's all about how you sell it: "Say: 'I had an amazing career doing X. I took time off to raise my kids. I pivoted into another career so I could balance everything. And now my kids are grown, I've got the time and energy, and I intend to have twenty more years of an amazing career.' When you own your story, everyone else will too."

Tell your story with confidence and a positive attitude.

But . . . don't let unrealistic expectations set you up for failure. Now for some really tough love from coach Liz Bentley: the key to a successful career transition or return is to start with a big, stiff reality check.

Yes, on the one hand, don't sell yourself short. On the other hand, Bentley says, she sees a lot of women who don't realize that pivoting a career or re-entering the workplace after a break in some situations can mean starting over. She sees that a key mistake women make as they're getting back into the job market is overvaluing what they did in a previous job and not accepting that they may need to restart at a lower level.

When you're restarting or pivoting, you may need to take a lower-paying job at first. You may even have to do some jobs for free, if the opportunity exists, just to get some recent and relevant experience on your résumé. You need to approach re-entry with the attitude that you have a lot to prove and knowing that, with the advantages of experience, you will rise much faster than someone who is starting out after just graduating from college.

"I am not saying you should undervalue yourself and take a job as a janitor. I'm not saying you shouldn't go for stretch jobs. I'm not saying you shouldn't put yourself out there. I'm just saying that you should recognize that the past is the past," Bentley argues. "[You have to come in thinking], *I've got a lot to prove. I can totally do it, and I will rise fast because I am talented and I've got a lot in my arsenal, but right now I just need to get in there, and I need to be willing to do a lot of stuff to prove myself.*"

And, yes, it's good to have a goal job, but play the long game. Know that the first job back or while in a pivot might just be a stepping stone. Bentley says she sees women dismissing job possibilities because the schedule isn't quite flexible enough, or the money is too low, or the opportunity isn't exactly what they were hoping for. If there's any way at all that you can make it work, say yes. Know that you will negotiate better terms once you have leverage—or you will move on to the next opportunity. "I see a lot of women saying no to things that they shouldn't say no to," says Bentley. "I see them put up barriers to things they shouldn't put up barriers to. Again, they will rise fast. That's not to say that they can't ask for their needs, but in a competitive environment, you need to prove yourself first. You can make a lot more demands once you are in the market and you've created your value."

By the way, this is also true for women who aren't starting over. As they say in television, you're only as good as your last show. I have to prove myself every day on *Morning Joe*.

Be ready and enthusiastic about proving your value all over again. This will not be forever. Say yes to those not-so-perfect opportunities, especially if they can be a bridge to your ultimate goal.

Don't quit when things get tough. As you experience the realities of job transition, there will be ups and downs, starts and stops. You will feel overwhelmed, discouraged, and down. Bentley says she sees people quit after one or two rejections. "Don't be afraid of the hard," says Bentley. "The hard is normal. It's about believing in yourself when no one else does. Surround yourself with people who champion you but also give you reality checks on your truth. And remember that grit is the number-one ingredient in all success stories."

Award-winning journalist Lisen Stromberg conducted "the most comprehensive modern survey of the career paths of highly qualified women" for her groundbreaking book, *Work Pause Thrive: How to Pause for Parenthood Without Killing Your Career*. She surveyed nearly fifteen hundred women—most of them with secondary degrees—on the impact of a career break on their professional lives. Seventy-two percent of the women Stromberg interviewed had paused or downshifted for a period of time to care for their families. Of those women, 85 percent have successfully relaunched. Stromberg says these "pauses" are part of the arc of a career, not the end of it.

"My headline: don't give up," she told Ginny. "What I found again and again in my interviews is the women who weren't thriving are the women who gave up. They bought into the narrative, *Oh, I'm not going to find a job*. And it *is* harder. You've been out of the paid workforce, and you want to boomerang back to your old career, or you're pivoting to a new career that's going to be really challenging. But don't buy into the narrative that it can't be done. Innovate a way that it *can* be done. Don't give up."

It may often be, she says, that women take a job that did not pay as much and didn't require as much time so that they could get back in a way that worked for them. But once they were back in, "Boom—within a year or two they had nailed it. They had moved to a new company, gotten a promotion, made much more money. I had one woman tell me, 'Two years in, no one even remembered I was out for fifteen years. It's like, What can you do for me today?' Once you get in, this will be a distant memory. You just have to commit to getting in."

Remember: celebrate every small win. There will be days when you have three steps back for each small step forward. It's okay to feel scared and to not have your sea legs and confidence every day. Everyone has been here. But you won't be here forever as long as you keep pushing yourself forward. To quote my favorite fish, Dory: "Just keep swimming."

Let your posse power your journey. A good support network is critical to anyone making a major career or life change. This is a bruising process, and you need people around you who believe in you, will encourage you—and will help hold you accountable.

Our friend Alicia Schober talks about her experience with the job search and the incredible resource she found in other women doing the same thing. At the beginning of her journey she didn't know anybody who wanted to return to work—many of her friends were either already working or wanted to continue managing their households. Then she signed up for a workshop for women re-entering the workforce. She was scared about making a big change and nervous about taking a step forward. "At the beginning of the workshop, we were asked to tell our story, why we took a pause," she says. "As I was listening to the other women I realized there were others like me. I was overwhelmed with the feeling that I am not alone in the journey. There was a cohort of women like me." She found workshops and groups who met a few times each month. She learned, made connections, and found people she could lean on when the search became tough. One woman started a job-seekers accountability group, and Schober eventually became the leader. They would practice interviewing, look at each other's résumés, and, most importantly, do an emotional check-in.

Ginny has a group of long-time close friends she relies on for support. They've raised their kids together, grown through their thirties and forties and now fifties together, been through job ups and downs together, and helped each other through crucial life moments. They don't all live in the same town anymore, but they are Ginny's vital support system and posse.

It may look like everyone around you is doing great—hello, Facebook feeds of perfect family moments . . . let's just call BS on that right now—but real life is just not that curated and perfect. At our age, now more than ever, we need friends and community. Make sure you have yours. Edit away the people who aren't completely supportive of your goals. Seek out people who are on the journey with you—or who can cheer you and bolster you along the way. Reach out and make new friends. Whether you are thirty-five or seventy-five, there is nothing better than laughing with your girl-friends. There is safety—and solace and much-needed support—in the girl squad. Gather yours—in person for a weekend, for a long walk, on the phone, on a group text . . . whatever works—and know that together, you got this.

Enough tough love and couch talk. Now I need to figure out what, exactly, I want to do . . .

4.

IT'S YOUR TURN NOW

Blue Sky Your Future

It's seven o'clock on a January morning in 2019 on the New York set of *Morning Joe*. Claire McCaskill is making her debut with us, just two months after losing her bid to return to the Senate representing Missouri for a third term. She has decades of political experience under her belt—she'd held statewide office in Missouri as state auditor for two terms and was elected district attorney of Kansas City for two terms and state representative for three terms. She's sixty-five, the matriarch of a large blended family, and a grandmother of twelve. And today she's starting all over again. And she can't hear a word Joe and I are saying because her wire is malfunctioning. She starts to wonder if this is a *Morning Joe* hazing ritual. But she laughs and makes it work because she's a pro.

Losing an election when you're an incumbent is the political equivalent of being fired with the whole world watching. Claire says it was tough ending her political career—election night and the days that followed were challenging. She had kept up a relentless pace in a very focused, decades-long career, and then suddenly that career was set aside and she "was confronted by the abyss." It was time to start over.

The big question is—for McCaskill and anybody else restarting a career at midlife: If you're not going to do what you've always done, what *are* you going to do?

"I think that's daunting for anybody," she says, but "for many women over sixty who still need or want to work, when there is a career change, it is a life change. It's scary.

"There is less time to make mistakes," she points out. "You've got to be really thoughtful about what you're good at, where you can succeed, why you can pitch your value to a future employer. It's not like you can say, 'I'll try this for five or six years, then I'll go try something else for five or six years.'"

Claire said there was no question that she wanted to keep working, and she was lucky in that television presented a natural transition. Certainly, she knew the ropes: talking on television is something she's done as part of her work for a very long time. Years of experience taught her how to speak directly and without artifice. And without a doubt she knows her subject: politics and the inner workings of Washington. She also knows a lot of people who work in television, including me and Joe, and everyone wanted her expertise. She says, "The phone started ringing, and that lifted me in so many ways. It lifted me professionally, obviously, but it also lifted me psychologically." News professionals and networks were calling, saying, "Hey, we want you to talk to us" and, "Hey, you need to make this happen!"

But most of us don't have companies banging down our doors, asking us to consider a new and different field when it's time to make a career change.

You may need a beat to figure it out. If you're not going to do what you've always done, then what? Obviously, if you've just been let go and you have no safety net, you may just go ahead and pursue anything and everything in order to support yourself. But if you have any freedom at all to take your time to find a job that not only earns money but also aligns with your interests and values—that's the challenge and the goal.

Licensed psychologist and author Guy Winch encourages women who have that freedom to view this time as an exploration: What do you really want to do with your life? Often, when people are faced with a field of options, they can't think of any one thing. Perhaps they haven't had a life's dream, the one thing that's their answer. He says it might be easier instead to think of ten things that might be sort of interesting. He encourages transitioners to think of this as "investigating what your interests are, going back to old ones that you never really had a chance to explore, discovering new ones, brainstorming. . . . It's easier to do when you are framing it as an exploration—a 'trying things out' stage—as opposed to a 'need to figure out the answer and devote yourself to it on spec' stage."

Look at your career transition as a process—and one you might even enjoy. A study by Pay Scale found that 82 percent of people who chose to make a career change after the age of forty-five did so successfully. It also found that many of them were happier and earning more than they had before. It *can* work. The key is to look for—and grab hold of—new opportunities to grow and learn.

It's your turn now.

Embrace the Adventurer Mindset

"Starting over is not for everybody," warns Lesley Jane Seymour when we told her we wanted to talk about midlife reinventions. "Let's be honest: it's freaking hard. You have to be an explorer and an adventurer to want to start over in your fifties and sixties. Some people will think it's great. Others will look at it with horror."

For eight years Seymour was the editor-in-chief of *More* magazine. She'd had a long and successful career in the magazine business, helming *Marie Claire*, *Young Miss*, and *Redbook*. But she saw that the writing was on the wall for herself and the publication after experiencing a revolving door of bosses and publishers.

"When my fifth boss sat me down and asked me what would happen to the beauty advertising at the company if they closed *More* . . . I don't really remember what he said after that. I was like, *Okay, I understand where this is headed.* It took three years for them to close it, but I'm not stupid. I got it. That was when I went and asked myself, *What other things have I missed in my life that I've always wanted to do?*"

Seymour reached back to her college days at Duke, where she'd loved her marine biology classes. And, at the age of fifty-nine, she went back to school at Columbia at night to get her master's in sustainability, preparing herself for the pink slip she knew was coming.

Doing something completely different, she says, was terrifying—but invigorating.

"I like that feeling of *Holy crap, I don't know what I'm doing*, because that's when I feel like I'm growing. That's my personality: I like being put in those scary situations because I'll grow. It pushes me. I thought I would segue from sustainability over to the beauty business. That was my whole plan." Then, three years later, when *More* ultimately shuttered and her readers begged her to do something else for women over forty, Seymour ratcheted her class load back to one class a semester and started a new business, creating CoveyClub, an online magazine and community for the demographic.

"I have two tracks now—it's kind of wacko," she says. "This morning we're working on our capstone project on getting lead out of the drinking water for schools, then I have to switch and do something for CoveyClub on how to find the best bra. But I like the discordance of that. For me the friction of the discordance causes growth. I'm making an impact and changing people's lives."

It is about mindset—about saying yes and knowing that the way forward might not be a clear path or straight line.

"Success is in the way we approach our future," says corporate keynote speaker and "authorpreneur" Megan McNealy. McNealy is a successful wealth adviser at one of the top financial firms in the world. But in her forties, already suffering from two "incurable" autoimmune diseases, she also was diagnosed with cancer. She decided to start her own well-being protocol and ended up not only healing herself but also sparking her own personal and professional reinvention: McNealy now has a side career of inspiring workplace success through well-being, leads a vibrant online well-being community, and is the author of *Reinvent the Wheel: How Top Leaders Leverage Well-Being for Success*.

"The best reinvented people that I've seen—they are eager and excited, they don't know what awaits," she says. "They are moving forward in some way toward the clues that are laid out in front of them. They need to have a mantra of: I'm going to enjoy this process. I'm going to discover so much. Here I am, an adventure is going to unfold. I have no idea where this is going to lead me. I am just going to pick up the crumbs and I'm going to move forward."

Time for a Deep, Personal Dive

So many times it's the prospect—and opportunity—of an empty nest that makes us want to reshuffle the deck, as it was for Ginny. "I hear from so many of the women I work with: 'For the last twenty years I had a purpose, and that purpose just left the house,'" says ReBoot Accel's Diane Flynn. "They want to find something that provides meaning. We encourage them to think about not just what they can do or what they've done but what they want to do."

It's your turn now.

"This is your chance to grab something that is your own, something to sink your teeth into. Not just a hobby—something with meaning," says Grown and Flown cofounder Lisa Heffernan, whose powerhouse following is filled with women going through exactly this transition and who, along with her cofounder, Mary Dell Harrington, found her own unlikely second career when they created a little blog, Grown and Flown, for parents of teens and college-aged kids. (More on their story in Chapter 13, but spoiler alert: their blog's not so little anymore!) "Your first career was driven by money and paying student loans. You didn't know much about life. Your second career—you have a much greater knowledge of yourself. We know the world in a way we didn't before. Women find much more satisfaction in this second career."

Whether you are coming off a career break or a job loss or you're just restless and ready to jump ship, your first step in this adventure is to take a detailed personal assessment. You need to know your strengths and weaknesses—really know them. You need to have a clear idea of what you want and why, to understand what motivates and inspires you. You need to get a handle on what environment or culture you thrive in. In short, you need to become self-aware, beyond just knowing what you're good at. And you need to figure all of this out before you start launching your résumé out into the world.

Your next chapter may be completely different—and better!—than your career path in your thirties. The past decades of life experience, whether in or out of the workforce, may have altered your perspective and changed your values and priorities. Maybe you found that, after a career in accounting or communications, what you really love is giving your friends advice on interior design—and you're pretty good at it too, if you do say so yourself. Why not dig into that a bit and see if that path could work? Maybe you had a brilliant career in marketing, but your volunteer work has included fundraising or event planning, and you've found you have a knack for that. Where might that lead? Where might there be overlap between your previous skills and experiences and your newest passions?

"You may say, 'I want to go back to work or change jobs or industries,'" says Flynn of ReBoot Accel, but, she says, you need to dig further. "Maybe what you really want is fulfillment, or impact, or purpose, or income, or flexibility, or benefits." The better you understand what you need, the easier it is to identify your next career path and what you need to do to get there.

"It occurred to me that I was not at the right place." Knowing when it's time to leave a job or position is not easy, says former corporate executive, government, and communications pro Laura Cox Kaplan. "Once I reached a point in my career that provided me real financial stability and potential career longevity, I got comfortable. The flip side of a rural Texas upbringing that instilled in me determination, reliability, and a strong work ethic also taught me it was stupid to walk away from a sure thing. The problem was that sure thing had stopped challenging me in the ways I needed to be challenged." When her friend Sheryl Sandberg was writing a book urging women to "lean in" to their careers, she asked Kaplan to write about a time when she had taken a career or personal risk that paid off. Kaplan said that, in trying to write it, "I was struck that I had stopped taking the types of big risks that I had taken earlier in my career—the ones that helped me get from Rising Star, Texas, to the management team of a global professional services firm. I realized I hadn't done enough to challenge myself to live larger and to attempt to make a bigger contribution and impact. It was a wake-up call."

Laura went on to try to challenge herself more within her senior position at Pricewaterhouse Coopers, LLP, where she'd spent more than a decade. She began working on initiatives at PwC to close the gender gap in Congress, on both sides of the political aisle. But even with the support of the firm, she found she wanted more. "I realized I needed to push myself harder, potentially beyond the confines of my existing role, and to use my voice, perspective, and experience to have greater impact. I wanted to work on the issues that really lit me up inside."

After two years she ultimately separated from the partnership and is now an adjunct professor at American University, where she teaches personal and leadership development for women. She is the creator and host of the women- and leadership-focused podcast *She Said/She Said*. And she is making an impact on two corporate boards as well as several nonprofit boards (including Running Start, which encourages young women to run for elected office).

How did she end up finding the right direction? Kaplan says it took a lot of personal introspection. She had to consider what was working and not working for her and to evaluate all of her possible paths so she could figure out what was most appealing. She says she wouldn't have left without something to go to, even though, she says, where she landed was more of a mission than a job. Like many women at midlife, Kaplan wanted to contribute and have an impact. It took working with an executive coach, talking to friends and colleagues, and increasing her own self-awareness about what made her tick to help her find the right path.

What makes you want to leap out of bed in the morning? What gets you excited? If you are passionate about something, you're probably going to do well at it. As career coach Mary Beth Barrett-Newman of 2nd Career Consulting points out, "The things we liked in our duties, tasks, and responsibilities [at previous jobs] tend to be our strengths, and the things we don't like frequently are the things we are not so good at—and no one is going to hire you for your weaknesses."

So sit down—right now—and take out a pen and paper. Review the positions you've held and significant volunteer work you've done. Reflect back on what you accomplished, in both paid and unpaid positions, and write it down. Really think about your biggest wins, your most valuable experiences, and the skills you were most proud to have mastered.

Ask Yourself
- What motivates me?
- What functional skills and competencies do I have now?
- What common threads run through my jobs and volunteer work?
- What are my strengths?
- What are my weaknesses?
- What personality traits define me?
- What were my biggest professional successes?
- What characteristics earned me kudos at work?
- What have I been doing lately that I love? Why do I love it?

What parts of my past or current jobs, hobbies, things I've done do I enjoy the most? Then generate a list of ideas, no matter how wacky they may seem, of all the things you love to do, and see what themes emerge.

There are also the practical considerations: Are certain benefits more important than others? Is commuting time critical? The practical needs are vital, and most people don't take time to sit down and calculate them, and the result is that they end up in jobs they don't love or feel secure in.

Practical Questions to Consider
- Do I need a certain income? How much?
- Do I need flexibility? What's my ideal work schedule?
- Can I travel for a job?
- How much of a commute am I okay with?
- Do I want to work on a team or by myself?

- Do I want to work in an office?
- What's my ideal work environment?
- How much structure do I need?
- How much autonomy do I want?
- Do I have a preference for a big company or a small business?
- At the end of each day, do I want to leave my work at work?

Take all these ideas and brainstorm. Start with your values, interests, skill sets, and dreams. Think outside the box, and see what possible jobs, careers, and industries emerge. Map these out against your practical values, and see what you come up with, from jobs to entrepreneurial ideas.

Then test out some of your ideas: have coffee with someone in the field, try a class, have conversations with people who have careers similar to those on your idea list. "You can learn quickly whether it's for you if you prototype in this way," says career coach and ReBoot Accel cofounder Diane Flynn. Have a "bias toward action"—in other words, don't just think about it; have conversations, experiment, and try. These small experiments will help you refine your list or lead to further conversations and fine tuning.

Flynn says one of her clients started by saying she could work in technology because that was her background. She also had strategic corporate skills. Through discussions, however, they discovered that what she loved was interior design, but she did not want to work with clients. Through the brainstorming process, they married up the client's interior design interests with her strategic corporate skills and came up with jobs that included working at Houzz or Pinterest in a strategic capacity.

It's like a Venn diagram of interests, finding careers in the overlap between your skills and passions. Or think of it like a board that Olivia Pope from *Scandal* would put together to investigate a crime, but you're investigating your next career move.

Find Your Secret Sauce and
Play to Your Strengths

Let's talk a little about the science of how your brain works when it comes to finding your strengths. Maybe you've been told to work on improving your weaknesses—I know I got that all the time growing up. But that's the wrong approach, says coach Liz Bentley. "If we were to look at our brain as a tree, and we said that the right side of the tree was our strengths, when we work on that side, the branches grow, the leaves grow, the flowers grow—everything lights up, and it lights up so much that it starts to creep over to the left side of the tree and diminishes our weaknesses. By working on our strengths, not only do we improve those strengths, but we can also turn our weaknesses into strengths and diminish those weaknesses. Now, conversely, if we are to work on our weaknesses, in our tree analogy the strength side doesn't grow, doesn't flourish, and the weakness side stays the same as well."

Plus, focusing on our weaknesses can make us feel insecure, which defeats the whole purpose. Sure, we need to recognize that we all have weaknesses and to know what they are. But how you are going to be great is by understanding and leaning into your strengths. Do you know what yours are? What's your secret sauce? Or, as Bentley likes to ask: What's your magic? What makes you really special? Everyone should be able to answer that question. Everyone should be able to say, "In my job the thing that I can do differently that other people can't, is *this*: I can have empathy with even the hardest of circumstances." Or, "The thing in my life that I've always been able to do differently is *this*: I can listen to someone's story and pull out the most important facts quicker than anyone else."

Then you need to be able to answer: Why does it matter? Perhaps it is: "I am really good at articulating my point to all kinds of people so that they can listen and we can work together and get things done." You want to look at intellectual skills as well as personal skills. How do your strengths impact all the people around you? How will they improve an organization? Even with artificial intelligence, there is one thing that is never going to change: we are never going to stop working with people. So an ability to understand and work with people is paramount to success.

And remember your historical wins? They are likely connected to your strengths. Talking about them in an interview, on a résumé, or in your LinkedIn profile will highlight your strengths and show what makes you special. Once you really understand, own, and articulate your strengths and know why they are valuable, you will be better at work, job hunting, interviewing, and pulling together your résumé and your LinkedIn profile. It will help you understand where you are on the map.

Ask for Input

You can do this deep personal dive on your own or with your squad, a career coach, or sometimes your college (alumni) career office.

A good career coach can help you figure things out. Career coaches are an unbiased third party and have no preconceived notions about you. They are going to know what is required in today's job market to find that position and help navigate you through the dos and don'ts of applying for it. There are executive coaches, like Liz Bentley, Mary Beth Barrett-Newman, Carroll Welch, and Diane Flynn, who advised us for this book, some of whom specialize in working with women who are transitioning back to the workforce or pivoting careers. They don't need to be local; many coaches work through FaceTime or Skype. You can find career coaches through LinkedIn or through word of mouth. (See our Resources section to find some of the organizations that have career coaches on their teams.)

Many coaches will use psychological tests, and you can try some of these on your own. There are a number of online tests you can take to analyze your personality, strengths, and skills and how that relates to a career, like CliftonStrengths. There's also the Myers-Briggs test (MyersBriggs.org), which can help you figure out your personality type and what kind of career you are best suited for, or the O*Net Interest Profiler (MyNextMove.org), which can help you think of what kinds of careers you might want to look into (see the Resources section for more). The benefit of doing these tests is that they give you language to talk about your talents and strengths in addition to showing you what types of roles you would do well at. Sometimes they uncover strengths you didn't realize you had.

Ginny tried CliftonStrengths (you can buy the book on Amazon and get a code for a free thirty-minute online test) and found that her five most "dominant themes of talent" are Individualization (she is "intrigued by the unique qualities of each person"), Input (she is "inquisitive and collects information"), Learner (she "loves to learn"), Responsibility ("always dependable"), and Communication (she likes to "explain, describe, host, speak in public, and write"). The idea behind CliftonStrengths is that instead of trying to correct your weaknesses, if you can identify your top talents and turn them into strengths, you will perform well.

Ask Your Friends and Family What They Think

Some people feel a career services professional can offer the best advice; others feel more comfortable closer to home, asking family and friends for their opinion of how their strengths might be best applied.

Broadcasting legend and former *Today Show* host Meredith Viera has managed to successfully reinvent her career a number of times.

Meredith says that when she is trying to figure out her next steps, her first move is to gather her posse. "What I recommend is to choose friends and people that you trust, and bounce ideas off of them. So often you don't see yourself the way someone else does. I talk to my friends about where my head is. I call them 'mini summits'—they are usually walks. We talk about things like, 'I don't know that I want to go back to what I was doing before, so how can I use all of my skills to do something that will really excite me now?'"

When I was out of work, I did this to some extent. I had discussions with my family and friends as well as my agent. Ginny has had talks with friends and family about new business ideas that use her background and skills. She has several buckets of experience—political communications, real estate, writing, and now women's career advice. My brother Ian, who knows her best, has told her that she needs to get back into politics and policy, either on a campaign, in a Hill office, with a mission-driven organization, or at a policy think tank.

The point is that sometimes other people can see us better than we see ourselves. They don't necessarily know the reasons you've decided you're not right for a particular career; they see only that you have obvious aptitudes and interests, so why not focus on them? Sometimes an outside perspective makes all the difference.

Career coach Barrett-Newman says, "You can start asking questions like, 'If you were in my shoes, what kinds of opportunities would you be looking at?' . . . They might say, 'Have you thought about being a project manager or working on a political campaign?' If you ask enough people those kinds of questions, people are going to start saying things that will make you think, *That sounds interesting—maybe I'll look into that.*"

You may be surprised at what people come up with. Ginny's friend Jill had spent more than a decade managing brands for some of the top companies in the country, working seventy to eighty hours a week and traveling three to four months a year. After becoming a mom, Jill tried job sharing and to find part-time marketing work, each to no avail. "Then someone said, 'Why don't you just try teaching?' I thought, 'I have never taught anything. I have no skill for teaching.' They said, 'Just try.'" Jill reached out to two local universities that said, "Yes, we'd love to hire you!" She started as an adjunct professor. "The first time I stepped into a classroom," she says, "I thought, *This is a part of myself I never knew I had.*" Jill had found her second calling and now lectures at a top business school. Jill's advice? "Don't try to recreate the career you had before kids. It's probably not feasible. Think about what else could be. I never imagined myself as a teacher. It was never part of my career plan. Any survey or assessment probably would not have shown me that path. But it's important to be open to different opportunities. I don't think that careers progress linearly. Think about each step in your career as opening up lots of different doors, not just the next door. I still think I might have a different career out there after this. Be open to serendipity. Be open to opportunity and trying things you're not good at. Taking risks leads to opportunities later."

Pull All the Pieces Together

That's exactly what our friend Alicia Schober did when she decided it was her time to return to work after an eighteen-year career break. She did some serious thinking and research about herself and the job that would be her best fit.

To figure out what she wanted to do, Alicia went through what she called the *discernment phase*. She spent six months exploring what was most important to her and how her skills would fit in. She participated in workshops, immersion classes, and job-seekers groups. She hired a career coach who had her go through a period of introspection, during which she explored her values. She took personality tests, and when she got the reports back, she highlighted commonalities of what they said her strengths were. She worked with a recruiter who was able to tell her where she would fit in today. Alicia wanted a job in corporate social responsibility, but the recruiter told her that, based on her skill set and experience, she should find a program management job. By spending time doing this deep dive, she was able to find a role that is a beautiful match of her experience and strengths: Alicia's now working as a program manager in a sales department. "I'm not in sales, but adjacent to it—instead, I'm improving processes and creating efficiencies. I am using my talents to work with lots of different people, taking programs from creation to completion. It is perfect for me."

Erica Galles had worked in marketing in the pharmaceutical industry, but after becoming a mom she had dialed back her work to part-time consulting for twelve years and then took a career break for five years. As she prepared to return to work, the mom of three teenagers also wanted regular hours. Erica sought guidance from Flynn of ReBoot Accel, who helped her figure out what she wanted to do and where she could do it. Flynn helped Erica refine her thoughts on her likes and dislikes based on her previous roles and projects. They were able to create a primary career objective that focused on function (organizational, project based, strategic) rather than title (e.g., project manager). This different approach to a career objective can help surface careers that you may not have considered before but may nonetheless be an excellent match. Erica is now happily working as an office manager for JetBlue Tech Ventures, a venture capital subsidiary of JetBlue Airways. The venture capital and travel industry are both new to her, which Galles said she loves because she learns something new every day. By doing a deep dive and figuring out her strengths, Galles realized that she could bring her organizational skills to her new job.

ROADMAPS, PLAYBOOKS, AND GRIDS
TO HELP YOU FIGURE IT ALL OUT

For returners: **The iRelaunch Roadmap**. This structured, five-phase, on-line program includes podcasts, community forums, and articles to guide returners through the process. Find it on iRelaunch.com.

For the restless and pivoters: **The Landit Career Playbook**, a "personalized playbook for women seeking to move their career forward. Your personalized playbook will successfully guide you with access to world-class experts, resources, tools, coaching, and opportunities." Find opportunities, create your personal brand, assemble your "board of advisors," and get advice. Go to landit.com.

For anyone: **The Muse Grid**, found in the book *The New Rules of Work* by Alexandra Cavoulacos and Kathryn Minshew, helps you "sift through and narrow today's ever-growing menu of job and career options, using the simple step-by-step Muse Method."

Like Jill, Alicia, and Erica, you may need to envision yourself in a way you never imagined. Think about what you still want to learn and do, then figure out how you can connect your skills with that field.

Research the Field and the Job Market

Once you've done your own self-analysis, you'll need to figure out what's out there. The job landscape has changed dramatically in the past decade and exponentially in the past twenty years. As one coach told us, "You don't know what you don't know." If it's been a while since you last looked, you may be surprised by the career possibilities in your interest areas.

Start with a Google search. Check out the top companies in (what might be) your new field. Give yourself time to really search their websites and look at their job listings. Drill down into the kinds of services those companies provide, their job listing requirements, the bios of top employees, and other things that may offer perspective into the industry and job roles. Doing this research can provide insight into whether your priority list matches up with the company (e.g., flexibility or no travel or the ability to move up).

Naturally, social media is huge when it comes to researching jobs and industries. Facebook, Twitter, LinkedIn, Instagram, YouTube, podcasts, TED Talks—there is a prolific amount of information available through the social sites. If there are companies you are interested in working for, you can follow them on LinkedIn, Twitter, and even Instagram to keep up with the latest company news and developments. Specifically, research people and specific jobs on LinkedIn. Look at the profiles of people who have jobs similar to the type of job you want. Look at their skills, backgrounds, and experience. Where do you overlap with them? Where might you need to fill in?

You can get behind-the-scenes information by looking at websites like TheMuse.com, Glassdoor.com, and Fairygodboss.com for their insider company reviews that give insights into jobs, salaries, benefits, and company culture. Glassdoor, for example, has reviews on six hundred thousand companies. You can do a deep dive on your target company or industry or even see what types of jobs are available in specific cities. Enter a job title into the search form, and Glassdoor will suggest "Featured Jobs," "Similar Companies," and "Related Job Search" to help widen your net. In addition, Glassdoor has CEO approval ratings, salary reports, benefits reviews, salaries, and even office photos. Fairygodboss is specifically geared toward women and gives the inside scoop on pay, corporate culture, benefits, and work flexibility, with real reviews from more than twenty-five thousand women. The site posts job listings filtered by company, category, and location. Search salaries by both title and company.

You can also look at the US Department of Labor's Bureau of Labor Statistics. It has a searchable database called the Occupational Outlook Handbook, which can be a useful brainstorming tool. You can search industries, investigate job titles, review similar occupations, and learn about pay and job outlook and requirements. You can also see the industry trade organizations, which may lead you to contacts and other key info.

Your alma mater's alumni career office is another resource when researching new careers. Some even have programs for alumnae who have taken a career break. Check out your university's website for more information.

Once you have a résumé together (see Chapter 7) and a goal, a good staffing recruiter or headhunter who understands the industry you are returning to can also help identify jobs appropriate for your skill set. High-quality staffing firms have the inside track and contacts, so they can get your name in front of the right people.

Embrace Your (Age) Diversity

A lot of companies today are recognizing the need for a more diverse workforce: they want not only more women but also more "grown-ups" and "age diversity." Tami Forman of Path Forward helps women restart their careers after time spent focused on caregiving. She works with companies like Walmart, Netflix, Apple, NBCUniversal, and others to create midcareer internships. She cites Volta Charging as an example of a company that partnered with Path Forward to create paid return-to-work internships (for more on returnships, see Chapter 10) in their California headquarters. Volta says the "returnships" were a win for Volta Charging as well, saying the returners enhanced their team with diverse ideas and created an environment of growth and learning.

Forman observes that when companies stop focusing on the perceived disadvantages of a candidate who has taken a career break or is over forty, they begin to see real advantages in hiring someone with a prior professional track record and a wealth of life experience.

Companies may also just be tiring of catering to Millennial culture. "They are going to be willing to hire someone at fifty-three because they are sick of the entitlement and immaturity of the younger workers," says coach Liz Bentley, who often counsels managers to hire older applicants and returners, using their age as a selling point. "It's all about selling. You can really pitch yourself from the work-ethic standpoint and show why older is better: 'I am mature. I'm willing to do all this stuff. I've got wisdom. I've got work discipline. I'll stay here until the job gets done. I get responsibility, and I'm gonna make it happen. I have the creativity and flexibility to get stuff done.'"

Start Reaching Out

Don't keep your job search a secret. Start talking to people about your desire to go back to work or the pivot you want to make. As Diane Flynn says, have a bias toward action. Grab someone for coffee who holds a job you admire. When you go to a holiday party or a social event and someone asks what you are doing, Flynn says, you should jump on the chance to get the word out: "Use that as an opportunity to say, 'I'm so excited. I'm going back to work and pivoting careers, and here's what I am looking to do. Do you know anyone who I could talk to?'"

If you find a connection in your network who is in an industry or with a company that you think you may be interested in, reach out and ask if they will have coffee with you. Instead of saying that you are looking for a job, tell them you are returning to work or pivoting to a new area and that you are considering their industry or field and would like to learn about their insights. People are more likely to be helpful if they don't feel like you are inquiring about a job.

"It really is about doing informational interviews [more on those in Chapter 8] of people in those jobs, in those roles, in those industries to decide if it truly is interesting to you, to find out what kind of background they look for, and to see whether you are a fit for that kind of a position," says coach Barrett-Newman.

THIS IS YOUR TIME to blue sky your future. See how your strengths, current values, and priorities line up with opportunities in new and different fields. Take a structured approach to exploring new career possibilities, but stay open-minded and creative. Find a second or third (or fifth!) career that's your best one yet.

Now to position yourself for that next chapter . . .

5.

GET READY AND RELEVANT

Know Where You Are on the Map

Now that you have an idea of the industries, companies, and even jobs you want to target, there are a few other areas you may want to update and refresh before you launch your comeback. You need to figure out how to make yourself relevant and valuable to employers in that field. Even if you're not trying to explain away a career gap—maybe you're trying to pivot into a new field—you still could have holes to fill. You may have been fully employed for the past two decades, but your problem is pretty much the same: you're looking at a lifetime of experience and trying to figure out how to make sure you are relevant in a new or adjacent field.

And that's the key for everyone: you need to be *relevant*. As our friend Claire McCaskill puts it, "I feel an extraordinary pressure to always keep up with everything that's going on because I just don't want to be another pretty old face."

My best friend, Laura—who, at the age of fifty-one and after a thirteen-year career break and exhaustive job search, successfully returned to the same role in government relations in the energy industry—says that the most important thing she did was to keep up with her industry. She read annual reports, attended lectures, and signed up for daily emails from energy publications and research and policy institutes, subscribing to any leading organization in the energy industry. She read the *Financial Times* and the *Economist* and kept tabs on what was going on in her field globally and legislatively. This knowledge was critical for her when demonstrating her value to companies in the cover letters she would write, in framing her experience on her résumé, in her pitch, and, of course, in showing the people who interviewed her that she was current.

But the process was grueling. Even just to watch her go through it was tough. I have to admit that at times I really had given up on her ability to return to work because it just felt like the whole concept of her being involved in power issues and lobbying on Capitol Hill was for a younger person who had stayed in the game. (I was so wrong!) But she kept at it. She maintained her passion for energy policy during her decade in Connecticut and then upon returning to Washington by watching webcasts and reading trade papers. She kept pursuing opportunities, and she refused to give up. I'm so proud of her and happy for her. Her dedication and perseverance totally blew me away.

But she had to open a lot of disheartening emails to get there.

"Rejection after rejection. I've got a file of automated rejection letters. Many times, except for the career break, I felt more than qualified for the position." With an MBA from a top business school, Laura had worked for ten years in the energy industry at PPL, a Fortune 500 electric and gas utility. Five of those years she spent in business development, then five years in federal government relations. She left her job in 2006 when her daughter was two and her husband's career took them to Connecticut. Six years after her offramp, in 2012, she began her search to return to work, sending out résumés here and there. She was eager to get back into the energy industry with a role in government relations or business development, but the career break kept tripping her up. She thought a midcareer internship designed for professionals who took a break would be a natural transition back, and in 2014 she applied to the Goldman Sachs Returnship Program, but she was turned down. When her family moved back to DC in 2016 she amped up her search and began networking. "I had a number of informational interviews, but none of them led to a job."

Despite this, says Laura, networking—reaching out to former colleagues and friends in the industry as well as complete strangers—is an important step in the return process. "It's an important thing for anyone like me to do because eventually something will come up." In the midst of her re-entry she put the energy industry search on hold and worked for my mom, Emilie Brzezinski, as an art publicist, coordinating two major exhibitions of my mother's monumental tree sculptures. Laura is like a second daughter to my mom and knows and loves her art, so it was a perfect fit. "I was open to that because I wanted something fresh on my résumé. It was out of my targeted industry, but it was a great experience. I think it's important in a situation like this to say yes to opportunities, even if they don't necessarily align." When my mom moved to Florida in the fall of 2018 Laura renewed her job search, sending out résumés to energy industry openings she heard about through her network or found on job sites like Indeed.com. The automated rejections continued until, one day a few months later, she got an email from GE expressing an interest in a phone interview.

An HR recruiter at GE saw Laura's résumé and cover letter and wanted to learn more about her background, despite her career break. "She believed that you shouldn't automatically rule someone out because of a career gap," Laura says. It also turned out that the hiring manager with whom she would eventually work knew Laura from her time with PPL, so she had a contact in the DC office. Laura did an initial phone interview, then in-person interviews, each of which she spent days preparing for. She got an offer in June

2019 and began her comeback career in July as the director of US Government Affairs and Policy for GE Power—a similar role and industry she left back in 2006.

Laura says the key was persistence, a passion for the industry and the company, and staying in tune with developments in her industry and targeted companies. She advises that you follow companies or organizations that interest you like you already work there. "I was always preparing for the interview that might be. Read as much as you can about the company and field that interests you. Check relevant websites regularly. For example, about the time I was applying for my current position, the CEO of GE wrote his first letter to shareholders outlining his vision for the company. It proved so helpful in understanding the direction of the company."

Laura says she also spent hours attending industry events and watching webcasts like the World Economic Forum in Davos, Switzerland, from her home office in Connecticut. "Don't underestimate the value of passive research. It gave me a sense of being involved, even when I truly wasn't. It helped me stay on top of the conversation." When she finally got a chance to interview she was able to demonstrate how current and relevant her knowledge was and how valuable her previous experiences would be to the company.

Laura says this was a tough process, but she offers this advice: "Applying for jobs is hard. The rejections are depressing and discouraging. These companies don't know what they're missing out on when they don't even give someone with a résumé gap a shot. But don't give up. There will be a company or someone in HR— like there was for me at GE—who believes that the gap should not disqualify you. Know very well what you want to do, and know why you want to do it. Figure out how your past experiences can be applied to today's challenges. Persevere and keep up with your industry so you are ready for that chance when it comes along and you can shine."

BEYOND BEING CURRENT and updated in your field, getting recent experience on your résumé—whether it is pro bono work, a class, relevant volunteer work, or a project—sends a signal that you're industrious, engaged, and continuing to develop as a professional. It's also a great way to network in the field.

But how do you know what you're missing and where you might need to upskill? Take a look at the LinkedIn profiles of people who have jobs similar to the one(s) that interests you. What skills do they have? Make a list of their top skills, education, experience, and credentials so you have a full view of the ideal candidate for that type of job. Go through that list, and figure out where you need to upskill or fill gaps with classes, training, or volunteer work.

Once you've identified your gaps, then you can begin to fill them. Here's how.

Keep Up. Just like Laura did, know your area of interest, and get current in it. Be able to discuss the latest developments, articles, and people in your field. Find thought leaders in your industry on LinkedIn, and follow or connect with them so you have access to a constant newsfeed of relevant information. See who the thought leaders are following, and then follow *them*. Join industry groups that influential people in your field belong to. Sign up for Google alerts. This is where all the research you've done—and continue to do—comes in handy. It can help offset any biases against career gaps as well as ageism: "Subject matter expertise is the antidote to ageism," says iRelaunch's Carol Fishman Cohen.

Show Your Chops. The right volunteer work can significantly strengthen your résumé if it's aligned with your career goal. Try it in a place where nothing is on the line. Find projects that will enhance and update your résumé as well as expand your networks. For instance, Ginny wrote blog posts for the Know Your Value website and got involved with iRelaunch moderating panels at their conferences and joining their advisory board. Do you have a friend who has a small business for whom you could do a marketing project? Can you offer your (fill in your expertise here) chops to a civic organization in town? Or, like Laura did as my mom's art publicist, grab an opportunity to add something fresh to your résumé. These are projects that will enhance your résumé, bolster your credentials, and likely expand your network.

Even if an opportunity is unpaid or pays less than what you would like to make, think of it as a bridge back. iRelaunch's Cohen calls this "strategic" volunteering—not just bringing cookies or helping set up at a school event but substantive volunteering in a lane adjacent to your career target. For example, Ginny's friend Mary, a lawyer who had taken a multiyear career break, did legal research for her brother, a criminal attorney. This work helped bolster her credentials as she sought to get back into the workforce and also rebuilt her professional confidence. Where could you offer your marketing, social media, writing, accounting, legal, business strategy, or whatever services? Is there a community need or a nonprofit, small business, or startup that you could do a project for?

Ginny's friend Hallie used her MBA background to identify a strategic volunteering opportunity. The mom of two wanted to stay active and engaged and enjoyed many volunteering opportunities in her children's school as well as the flexibility they provided. However, as her kids got older, she was looking for volunteer work that would better tap into her business skills and help update her résumé. A nonprofit in DC called Compass helped her bridge the back-to-work gap. Compass (with locations also in Chicago and Philadelphia; see CompassProBono.org) assembles volunteer teams of professionals to provide pro bono guidance to local nonprofits on projects that involve strategic planning, funding strategies, board development, and marketing. Many Compass volunteers are women who have taken a career break and want to refresh their business skills, update their résumés, and use it as a launching pad back into the paid workforce. Compass liked Hallie so much that they hired her. She now works as director of consulting programs.

Another Compass volunteer, Susan Thaxton, had a background as a naval officer and a Harvard MBA. She had worked at GM for a few years, then took a career break when her husband's job moved her family. An alumni newsletter mentioning Compass caught her eye, and she ended up as a project leader for the nonprofit for five years. Susan says her time off from work had zapped her professional confidence, and her volunteer work helped bring it back. Susan also learned about how nonprofits work, their leadership structures, and their unique challenges. She is now vice president of programs for The Mission Continues, a nonprofit that matches veterans who are returning home and want to continue to serve with nonprofits in under-resourced communities.

Working for free obviously should not be a permanent solution. The goal is simply to get more recent and relevant projects on your résumé as well as to expand your networks while you are continuing to look for appropriate paid work. (See the Resources section for a list of volunteer organizations and clearinghouses that may have a good strategic volunteering opportunity for you.)

Try a Short-Term Project. You don't need to work for free, of course. You might also be able to find freelance work or short-term projects. We love Flexjobs.com for this. Founded by a woman who needed to find her own flexible work situation, the site lists hand-screened, remote, part-time, freelance, and flexible job postings, all of which are professional and résumé worthy. So even if you can't commit to a long commute or standard hours, there are ways to arm yourself with current experience. Don't give up!

Get Smart. Filling gaps in your résumé may also mean you need to brush up, "upskill," and get current. This can be as simple as taking free online classes to get your tech or industry skills up to date (see the Resources sections for a list of websites), or it can involve returning to school and getting a degree or certificate. If you can take a class with "a field study or a capstone project, that is ideal," says iRelaunch's Cohen. Getting real-world experience while studying exposes you to the people in the field so you can network as it also puts a recent project on your résumé. It also provides experience that you can discuss in an interview.

After a career break and a few years in graphic design, Ginny's friend Ann Horowitz decided in her forties that she was ready for a career pivot to historic preservation. She'd been in the field of trade association management for sixteen years before moving to the DC area and stepping out of the workforce for a few years to raise her son. She was craving a professional life again but realized she needed an update. She found a three-year master's degree program in historic preservation, a field she loved. Her coursework and capstone project exposed her to many people in her field. She wrote her thesis on protecting historic districts from sea-level-rise impacts, and it was one of the first times anything had been written on the subject in the United States. She came away with a degree, work products, and new networks. Her job search took just one month—she landed a position as an urban planner in the historic city of Alexandria, Virginia. "It was the first job I applied for after graduating. I am sure I got it as I had developed a relationship with staff in the Department of Planning and Zoning." And the career break? "It never came up in conversation or the interview, and I did not bring it up."

With Ann's new knowledge and up-to-date experience supporting her previous project management and communications experience as well as the connections she built through her classes and project, the résumé gap did not even matter.

For Ginny's friend Michelle deSilva, an online master's degree helped bolster her credentials in a new field. Michelle had been in financial services and private equity before off-ramping from the industry to raise her children. During this time she served on and chaired several large nonprofit boards in Kansas City, ranging from healthcare, theater, sexual assault, animal health, literacy, to marine science. These opportunities sparked an interest in the nonprofit world. "I decided to leverage these volunteer opportunities for a career in nonprofit and foundation management, and the online master's at Northeastern helped make me more credible." Now in St. Louis, deSilva works for the St. Louis Community Foundation and is involved with several nonprofits.

Not everyone is able to invest in a master's degree, of course. And you don't necessarily need a full degree; often a class or a lower-level certificate is enough to show you know the latest in a field. There are many less expensive options. The web is full of online classes, and colleges near you probably have certificate programs. Check out udemy.com, coursera.org, and MOOCs (massive open online courses) (see the Resources section at the end of the book for more). If you are considering a pivot, classes also give you an opportunity to try out your area of interest to see if it is a good fit.

But before you invest in any educational program, be sure to check the school's accreditation to make sure you're dealing with a reputable institution. You will also want to talk to people in your prospective field so you are confident that investing time and money in a degree or certificate is actually necessary. The goal is to update your knowledge bank, not break the bank, so do your research on how much—or how little—training you really need.

Get updated in tech. Get your teenager off her phone and have her give you a lesson in social media. If you don't have children, ask your younger coworkers or extended family and friends. You can also close your digital divide with an online class or find free classes at your local library. This way you won't give the goldfish look when someone mentions hashtags, Google Hangouts, or PowerPoint presentations. You need to be familiar with Slack, Zoom, Basecamp, the Google suite, and Skype. Because technology is constantly changing, it doesn't matter if you don't have a clue what was current five years ago—what's going on today or tomorrow is the only thing that matters. (See the Resources section for learning opportunities.) Before you tune out on tech, keep in mind: you've mastered a lot more than this in your time—tech is a cakewalk. And remember: you can Google virtually anything.

Be fearless about learning new things. More important than being updated in tech, employers want to know that you are intellectually curious, that you embrace new challenges, and that you have learning agility. They want someone who doesn't hesitate to sign themselves up to learn something new. "Relevance is earned by staying nimble and continually learning and growing," says ReBoot Accel's Diane Flynn. At your midcareer stage, although you have experience, you also need to be open to new ways of doing things and doing them collaboratively. Be fearless and always ready and willing to learn.

Now it's time for you to learn to tell—and own—your career story.

6.

FRAME YOUR COMEBACK NARRATIVE AND OWN YOUR STORY

Part of pivoting, restarting, or relaunching your career is being able to market yourself—to know and articulate what your value is and to communicate what you bring to the table.

Self-promotion is something that Ginny really struggled with as she was redefining herself. She is excellent at identifying and advocating for other people's strengths—getting her kids through the college application process, helping friends figure out what they are good at—but when it came to identifying her own skills and strengths, she stalled out. When she spoke with career experts and they would ask her to tell them where she excelled, many times she fumbled it.

This is a subject I have dedicated so much work to addressing: how women don't always feel comfortable talking about their strengths, and all too often they reflexively downplay them. Now is the time, if you haven't already, to reject any impulse to self-deprecate. Take all that career soul searching you've done and use it to articulate your career story. Succinctly identify the expertise you bring across multiple categories, and run a compelling thread through your jobs, experience, side hustles, and volunteer work. Then you've got to connect the dots from what your value is to the job you are seeking. That, girlfriends, is your career story.

And, as Liz Bentley says, you need to own it.

Sure, piece of cake, you say.

But bear with me. If you know and are able to articulate your value to others, you can more easily land that new job or step up in your career. Yes, it is especially hard if you have been on a career break or are pivoting. How do you figure out and effectively communicate your value to a potential employer when you may not even be confident of it yourself?

Identifying Your Personal Brand

I know you just did an eye roll over the phrase *personal brand*. Just like you, Ginny hates the word *brand* when it comes to people, but the truth is that everyone has a brand. Your brand is your reputation. It's what other people think of you. It's what they say about you when you leave the room.

"Everybody has a personal brand," says branding and marketing expert Dr. Jill Avery, a senior lecturer at Harvard Business School and friend of Ginny's. A personal brand, she says, is "how others perceive you. You don't own your brand. It lives in other people's heads."

It's not just for detergents or celebrities. Your personal brand is shorthand for who you are and what you stand for. You control it in the way you present yourself and what you do—in person as well as through your social media profile (more on that in Chapter 9). Your professional work and activities are just some of the things that communicate your brand to the world around you every day.

Strong brands have word association. Chanel is synonymous with luxury. Target is trendy bargains. Brooklyn is hipster. When people think of you, what do they think of? Investment expert? The cool mom? Reliable volunteer? Marketing pro? Leader in the community? Talented musician? All of the above? Personal branding also communicates values: What are you passionate about? What are your guiding principles? What are your core values?

Here's what a brand is not: it is not a job title. My brand is not cohost of *Morning Joe*. Nor is it author and founder of Know Your Value.

My brand is serious and fearless political journalist. I think the moment I established my brand at *Morning Joe* was when I burned the Paris Hilton story—I refused to read a fluff piece about the infamous socialite because it was not serious news. I ripped up the script, threw it out, and then picked up a scrap and lit it on fire. The story of my refusal to read trivial "news" went viral, and that action went a long way toward cementing my brand as a serious broadcast journalist who doesn't tolerate pointless stories. My brand value—what I offer to you—is that I get to the truth of what's going on in the political world and don't waste your time with BS.

My brand is also advocating for working women. I built that brand when I wrote my memoir *All Things at Once* and then again with *Know Your Value*, when I began the conversation about the importance of knowing your value as a working woman. My brand value in this sphere is that I help women know, grow, and communicate their value at work and in their everyday lives.

"Strong brands share brand value—which is the value you offer to another," says Katie Fogarty, a career communications coach and founder and CEO of the Reboot Group. She helps companies and professionals grow by sharing better career and brand stories. "Brand value—or career value—is the value you offer to another. I often use Marie Kondo as an example. People with strong brands are memorable, persuasive, and compelling because they go *beyond* simply communicating what they do—they clearly share the *value* they offer to others. None of us would really care about Marie Kondo if she were just tidying up her own perfect sphere. We care about her because she can help us bring order and spark joy in our own lives."

But if you are not Mika Brzezinski or Marie Kondo or Chanel or Target, why should you care about your brand?

Yes, why? And if it lives in other people's heads, how the heck do I change it if I don't like the brand that's living there?

To create a strong LinkedIn profile, pitch and win clients, grow your network, and enjoy a greater sphere of professional influence, you must have both a clear idea of what you do *and* the value you offer to others. And, Fogarty says, you need to be able to share it quickly, cogently, and powerfully. "Too many people simply tell you what they do—or worse, what they've done—and they fail to tell you *what they can do for you*," she says. "Connecting with your audience and sharing what you offer them is the key to succeeding at work, interviewing, and job hunting."

Okay, where do I start?

Get out your notebook again. Sit down with a list of every job you've had, and pull out a few key words that describe the work you did in each position. What do they all have in common? What are the themes? What is the narrative thread that stitches together your career—even if there's been a long career break?

Here's an example of how Ginny formulated her professional brand. She looked at her work history, which included communicating legislative policies on Capitol Hill, developing strategic political messaging campaigns, marketing houses, marketing her real estate business, social media content marketing, developing content for a women's career empowerment website, writing a book about women and careers, and then marketing that book.

While her jobs have varied considerably—from a press secretary to a realtor to a writer—there is a common theme throughout: her narrative thread is communications. In all of her jobs the common denominator has been some kind of communications work, whether it is marketing, advocacy, writing, or storytelling. She has marketed, spun, and advocated for legislative policy and political campaigns, marketed houses, and marketed her own small business, and now she's coauthored and marketed this book. Ginny's brand is that she is a communicator and storyteller.

If you are returning to work but in a different capacity or you've been volunteering, you need to try to find the transferable skills and weave them into a narrative thread. Your narrative thread can be the skills you offer, whether that's management or people skills or mentoring. You can think of your narrative thread as the skills and qualities that you bring.

Because your brand "lives in other people's minds," as Avery says, you may need to make some adjustments in specific areas. As you update yourself, get current in your field, and have conversations and network, your brand will begin to adjust as well. Your online brand will also be a big part of your brand repositioning (we'll get into that in Chapter 9).

And a note: if you've been living in yoga pants, you will need to rebrand your image by overhauling your clothing choices. It sounds superficial, but it matters. Presentation is an important part of your brand. Take my brand, for example. Some other networks encourage their female anchors to show as much leg and cleavage as possible. That's not my brand. You may not be in broadcasting, but how you present yourself becomes part of your brand in others' minds. And while she's been working on this book, Ginny has spent much of her time at home working in jeans and T-shirts, which is fine for writing a book from your kitchen table. But she'll obviously need to step it up when she is interviewing for jobs and even when she's having lunch or coffee with former colleagues. If she runs into someone who she wants to refer her, she wants to be taken seriously. She doesn't need to wear her interview clothes every time she goes to Trader Joe's, but she needs to be aware of at least looking put together. (More on style and appearance in Chapter 11.)

Figuring Out Your Brand Value

Once you figure out your brand, you'll need to identify and articulate your brand *value*—how your talents and skills can be useful to other people. This is the heart of knowing your value and how you answer the question: What do your skills, professional story, and brand do for other people? Why should other people care about your brand?

"Too often people are confused and think they should only be sharing information about their qualifications," says Fogarty. "They're not paying attention to what's truly critical, which is telling the listener the value that you offer to them, the difference your work makes. That's where the magic happens."

Your brand value is what you can do for somebody else. When you can convey that clearly, you can do anything. You can walk into a job interview and get that job. You can walk into a cocktail party and feel comfortable and confident and answer that horrible question, "What do you do?" You can grow your network, win clients, and expand your business. Being able to communicate your value is the heart of what people should be doing on LinkedIn, in interviews, or just in everyday conversation.

My brand: *I am a fearless political journalist and analyst.*

My brand value: *I find the political truth for you.*

(My other brand—and passion—is a mentor to women, and my brand value is that I teach them to know their value and communicate it effectively.)

MSNBC periodically conducts polls to assess my brand and brand value. The feedback we get helps me to make adjustments. You can do the same thing. Suss out your brand value by asking those who know you best. Poll current and former colleagues, industry peers, clients, friends, and family for their perspective on your professional value. Then fold their feedback into your messaging. Adjusting your brand is part of the transition as you return to work or pivot to a new field.

"You may need to reposition your brand to make yourself more valuable to potential employers," says Avery. "You need to translate all of your experience, paid and unpaid, and create a value proposition. Define who you are through the lens of what the employer needs. For example, not 'mom of two kids' but someone who ran a fundraiser that raised X dollars."

For employers, they want to know: What can you do for me?

If you're panicking about not being able to articulate your brand value, think of it as simply telling the employer what you have to offer them and how you can help them. It doesn't need to be hard. You are just finding a way to talk about your career history and your strengths as they relate to a potential employer's needs.

Developing Your Pitch and Brand Statement

Once you've figured out your brand and brand value, you want to spin that into a pitch that explains what you bring to the table, what makes you unique and better—and tells someone why they should hire you.

Your pitch is not one size fits all. It will depend on the situation and audience. You'll use versions of it in conversations, in interviews, on social media, in your résumé, and as part of your LinkedIn profile.

Your pitch should be clear and well structured, and you should come across as motivated. You don't want to appear vague or wishy-washy. People can't help you if they don't know what you are looking for, and they probably won't want to help you if you don't seem enthusiastic.

This pitch is what you say when someone asks: What do you do? Or: What have you been up to lately? Those questions are now a golden opportunity for you to start getting the word out about your new plan. So hone your professional story to just a few simple sentences—with no jargon. Then practice saying it out loud. A lot. Record yourself with your phone until you look, feel, and sound comfortable.

Okay, now it's your turn to give it a try.

Have a Short and a Long Version

You want at least two versions of your pitch: a short, one-sentence, conversational, nice-to-meet-you-in-line-at-Starbucks pitch and your four-sentence interview or networking event version. Craft your longer, interview version first, then edit it down to a concise sound bite for a more informal conversation.

HOW TO DEVELOP
YOUR COMEBACK CAREER PITCH

Step 1: Share what you do—your brand.

Find that narrative thread that runs through your career, past jobs, and volunteer work.

"I'm a _____. I spent X years working in X field."

If you are currently doing volunteer or pro bono work and it is relevant to the field or job you are targeting, lead with that, then follow with your past experience.

"I'm a _____. Currently, I am volunteering my X skills at the pro bono clinic in town. I spent twelve years in X field, specializing in X . . ."

If you are doing something now that is not relevant to the field you're pursuing or if you are pivoting, is there anything that you are doing now that is transferable to the field you are targeting? Find that narrative thread.

Ginny: I'm a storyteller. Right now I'm writing a book about midlife women reinventing, rebooting, and pivoting careers. I have fifteen years of experience in strategic communications and advocacy, including more than a decade on Capitol Hill as a press secretary.

Step 2: Communicate the value you offer to others.

Answer the "so what?" question. What can your skills and expertise do for them? What makes your value more compelling than the competition's? If your audience is a potential employer, articulate how your value, skills, background, and expertise can help them.

Ginny: I can help you tell your story—whether it's about a political candidate, product, legislative initiative, issue, or business—in a way that will persuade, teach, or inspire.

(continues)

Step 3: Give proof—share your accomplishments.

When you are in an interview, list your accomplishments using facts and data.

Ginny: I've worked as a press secretary on Capitol Hill distilling complicated legislative initiatives into compelling copy and talking points. I've been a realtor and marketed and sold homes that were not always an easy sell. I've successfully branded and marketed my own real estate business. I've written an award-winning grant proposal for a public elementary school as well as thousands of press releases and blog posts, and now I've coauthored and marketed a book.

Step 4: A call to action—conclude with what you want.

If you are speaking with someone about something specific—like a job— the call to action is where you say that you want the job. After setting the stage with your professional story and stating your value, end with your ask.

"Now I am looking for something that will connect my X skills and interest in X, such as a position at X company."

Ginny: I would like to leverage my years of experience into a communications position either working on Capitol Hill, on a campaign, or for a nonprofit, think tank, or advocacy group.

Practice, Practice, Practice

Practice and refine it with your close friends and family. Say it out loud. Get feedback. Record it with your smartphone and play it back for yourself. At first it may sound strange and unnatural. Then, after you've practiced it out loud a few dozen times and refined it, you'll begin to believe it and get better at discussing it. Talking about it even helps you to sort through your ultimate objective for your pitch, like what you want to do and why you would be good at it.

NOTE FROM GINNY

Believe me when I tell you that this exercise may not feel comfortable at all. I felt weird even writing the sentences about myself, never mind saying them out loud! I had complete imposter syndrome and could not find a natural way to say any of it. But just practicing it conversationally with friends until it feels more natural will really help. You are not necessarily going to spit your pitch out verbatim in the course of conversation—that would definitely sound weird. But you do need to be able to articulate what you're good at and how you can add value to an organization—that's how you're going to succeed. So bite the bullet and do it. It is an important exercise to go through, and it will take a while to say anything like it without bursting out laughing or feeling like a robot. Do this with friends. They can help you adjust it and laugh with you—or, in my case, *at* you. Good luck!

7.

REFRESH, REALIGN, AND REBOOT YOUR RÉSUMÉ

If it's been a while since you last updated your résumé (for weeks Ginny literally could not even find her résumé, asking, "Who needs a résumé in real estate?!"), prepare yourself for a big revamp. Gone are the "job objectives" that headed up résumés a decade ago. Employers don't care about your objectives—they want to know what you can *do* for them. And, of course, technology has changed everything. Candidates are submitting résumés online, so your résumé needs to stand out from hundreds and grab the attention of the hiring manager. Your résumé now is a dynamic document that should be tweaked for each job you apply for—really. And regardless of industry, you may benefit from creating an online portfolio (*What?!*).

And yes, you need a résumé even if you're on LinkedIn. You absolutely still need to have a polished résumé and cover letter prepared to catch the eye of your target audience: hiring managers.

Your résumé is your pitch on paper. But unlike your pitch, your résumé doesn't have you there in person to sell it . . . until the interview. Think of your résumé as a selling tool to get someone interested in talking to you further about a job. And it's not a "tattoo," as one expert told us: you should be tweaking it (honestly) to every job you are targeting. It needs to show your value and fit for that specific job. It needs to show what you can do for the employer. It should be based on what you want to do next and showcase accomplishments with quantifiable data, not just a bullet point list of all your past jobs. It needs to include key words that echo the job description. It needs to be easy to read or scan, and for most people it should be max two pages.

And here's a sobering statistic. While you may spend a week perfecting your résumé for each job you target, the HR folks who receive it will spend on average less than twenty seconds scanning it, according to Sheila Murphy of FlexProfessionals, a DC- and Boston-based recruiting and staffing firm. Your résumé needs to sell you—and *fast*—before the person reading it moves on to the next one.

"Everything in life is about standing out," says coach Liz Bentley. "When you are returning or pivoting, you are trying to create credibility. You are up against a sea of candidates, trying to be picked out of dozens of heads. Why pick you?" What about your résumé, your LinkedIn profile, your pitch makes you special, interesting, different, credible, and the right match for the job?

Your mission: in one (or two) perfect pages show why you are best for the job.

If, like Ginny, you've zigged and zagged a bit in your professional life or if you've been out of the paid workforce for more than a few years, how do you make a compelling e-doc sales pitch out of a mash-up of careers, volunteer work, and an off-ramp? How do you get a potential employer to focus on what you can do for them— and how you can do it better than the competition—rather than your years out of the paid workforce?

Or, if you are pivoting careers, how do you repurpose the experience on your résumé? How do you identify and fill any holes? How do you explain a layoff? What do you do with past jobs that may not be relevant to your chosen field?

We asked the experts. Here's what we found out.

Make Your Résumé Gap Less Glaring

Anyone looking for a job after a career break is wracked with anxiety about explaining the years off—the dreaded "résumé gap." And with good reason. "You cannot leave time unaccounted for on your résumé," says iRelaunch's Carol Fishman Cohen. Nor do you want the most recent experience on your résumé to be from years ago.

Great, but that's my reality. What do I do?

Reframe what you did while you were out of the paid workforce. You probably haven't just been sitting around doing nothing. The activities you have been involved in—volunteering, pro bono work, taking classes—likely have valuable elements you can showcase for a potential employer. If there are parts of these activities that are relevant, include them. Murphy of FlexProfessionals says, "No employer is going to hire you because you have a gap, but they will hire you for the skills you sharpened or learned during your gap. Adopt your prospective employer's mindset and ask, 'What skills do I have that would be useful to this employer?' Highlight these with confidence, using concrete examples, and minimize other aspects of your gap that may distract."

Again, spotlight appropriate volunteer work and relevant continuing education, freelance projects, and conferences you have attended. Dig deep to recall the roles you have held over the years—both paid and unpaid—as well as the scope of your responsibilities and how you made a difference. If you are coming up short, you may need to pick up a course or find some relevant volunteer work to freshen up your résumé, as we discussed in Chapter 5. You could do some freelance projects, teach an after-school enrichment course, lead a technology committee, or help out a small business. But remember: "Don't exaggerate or falsify your experience," says résumé expert Tamara Dowling of SeekingSuccess.com. The truth will come out, either in the interview or elsewhere.

Lisa, who went back to work after more than a decade home with her kids, says she took all of her volunteer work and reframed it as "project based," and then she talked about it in terms of results—money raised, time saved, lives impacted. "I put it in business terms," she told us.

Returner Alicia Schober took a similar approach and put her volunteer work under the Experience section of her résumé. Alicia had championed bringing an all-inclusive playground to her city. She had pitched the idea to her city council and county board of supervisors and helped the idea get traction in her hometown. She had also served on her homeowners' association board and her local elementary school board. The career coach and recruiter she was working with advised her that her civic work showcased her project management skills and should be there. She called it "Civic Experience" and described it in business terms. Her civic experience, although unpaid, showcased what she could do, and in the end, Alicia says, it helped to get her hired.

If you were out of the paid workforce, you may not be able to cite accomplishments in a tidy list under a job title, but like Alicia and Lisa, you can group projects in ways that make sense and highlight your skills and accomplishments. Just because your achievements were unpaid does not mean they should not be on your résumé.

And now, the nuts and bolts of how to put all that on paper . . .

Structuring Your Midcareer Reboot Résumé

Let's preface this by saying there are many ways to format a résumé. And, of course, types of résumé will differ by industry and level of expertise. There are more traditional formats, there are infographic résumés, and there are even video résumés. Google "résumé template," and you can find all kinds online. You can probably find templates in your word processing software as well. You will want your format to be industry appropriate (e.g., skip the infographic format for that banking career). Within that framework you want it to look updated, modern, and fresh. Experts say the best fonts today are Calibri, Helvetica, and Arial. You want it to be readable—make sure there is white space, and don't make that font smaller than 10. And when you send it, export it as a PDF so it doesn't get wacky in translation. In addition to those basics, from speaking with experts, we learned there are a few things that most résumés today should include and best practices if you are returning, pivoting careers, or simply are LFAJWF+ (looking for a job while fifty-plus). So if it's been a while since you last put together a résumé, fasten your seatbelt.

For a visual reference, we've included a basic résumé as an example. Remember, though: every situation is different.

The Headline

This is a branding document, so treat it that way. Use every opportunity, from style to tone to content, to showcase your brand and brand value. That includes the most visible part of the document—where your name and contact information reside.

Make your value obvious right away to that rushed, twenty-second résumé reader. Start at the top: consider adding a term or two under

First name Last name
City, State

123.456.7890
yourname@server.com
your LinkedIn address here
@yoursocialhandles

Your headline or tagline here.

"You can put a quote from a reference here."

PROFILE

Your one- to three-sentence statement that shows why you are the right person for the job. This needs to sizzle and not just repeat your resume. Think about tweaking it for each job.

CORE COMPETENCIES

A bulleted paragraph style list of your skills and expertise. These words should mirror words in the job description. Keep it honest and adjust for each job as necessary.

EXPERIENCE

COMPANY or ORGANIZATION, City, State

Job Title (year–present)

Several-line description of your job responsibilities.

- Accomplishment with data and/or PAR
- Accomplishment
- Accomplishment

CAREER BREAK (year–year)

Took time off from work to care for my ailing father/raise my children/take care of my sick spouse.

COMPANY or ORGANIZATION, City, State

Job Title (year–year)

Several-line description of your job responsibilities.

- Accomplishment with data and/or PAR
- Accomplishment
- Accomplishment

COMPANY or ORGANIZATION, City, State
Job Title (year–year)
Several-line description of your job responsibilities.

- Accomplishment with data and/or PAR
- Accomplishment
- Accomplishment

COMPANY or ORGANIZATION, City, State
Job Title (year–year)
Several-line description of your job responsibilities.

- Accomplishment with data and/or PAR
- Accomplishment
- Accomplishment

EDUCATION

University, City, State
Master's, Subject (Year)

College, City, State
Bachelor of Arts, Subject (Year)

PROFESSIONAL DEVELOPMENT

Annual Conference Workshop, description (date)
University, Graduate Seminar, description (date)
Certification in Relevant Skill, description (date)

AFFILIATIONS

Society of Relevant Field (date–date)
Board Member, Organization (date–date)

TECHNICAL SKILLS

List appropriate programming or industry specific skills here.

your name that describes your brand, such as: Communications Pro or Leadership Consultant or Civic Leader or Biotech Professional or Digital Content Expert or Global Marketing Communications or International Education Leader or Community Organizer.

Or you can go a little further. Returner Alicia Schober came up with a tagline that she placed under her name and that wove together her civic work with her business background: *Strengthening communities by bridging corporate and civic know-how.* She then added three key strengths from both her paid and unpaid experiences: *Civic Leadership | Community Development | Marketing & Sales Management.*

Also at the top, your social media handles join your name, phone number, city, state, and email address. As part of your branding strategy, social media addresses will send the important message that you are current. LinkedIn today is a non-negotiable, so get your profile together (Chapter 9) and put its URL on your résumé. If you are active on Twitter and you tweet about topics that are relevant to the job you are seeking, your Twitter handle should be on there as well. Same goes for Instagram and even Pinterest if you are in a visual field. Facebook is usually more personal, so it's probably best to leave that off. If you have a website, include that here as well.

Make sure your email address sounds professional, not Mollies Mama@aol.com. The use of an unprofessional email address can actually get a résumé rejected out of hand. Best to have firstname lastname@server.com. If you are currently employed, don't use your work email. And ditch the AOL address for the job search—HR experts say that address sounds outdated.

The Profile

The professional profile or summary is the most important part of your résumé. If you are coming off of a career break or pivoting, including highlights or a summary at the top will boost your résumé. This is your brand marketing message, giving the reader a thumbnail sketch of your brand value. Do not waste this space by simply regurgitating your résumé.

"The 'profile' needs to tell the employer—quickly, concisely, and with a little sizzle if you can—what you bring to the table," says Sheila Murphy of FlexProfessionals. "Having a good profile is critical because an employer may read nothing else but your profile, so it must nicely summarize what you can do for them. For returners, the profile is a great way for you to indicate an eagerness to re-enter or to let the employer know that you are looking to transition to something different."

Your profile proclaims in about fifty words why you are an excellent match for the job at hand. "Without a profile, a résumé is not framed with a purpose," says résumé expert Tamara Dowling. As with the rest of your résumé, this section is dynamic—what you choose to highlight here may change with different job applications. The profile makes your suitability for the job immediately evident, helping employers focus on your value, not your age or career gap. Keep it to one to three sentences, either as a statement or in bullet points that define your value. Show why you are better than the competition, what your strengths are, and why people want you on their team. For those pivoting or if you have a lot of various experiences, this summary is a chance to weave everything together in a way that may not be apparent from your résumé. You can highlight your transferable skills or knit a common thread through a variety of different experiences.

Have you won awards in your career? Say it here: "Award-winning editor." Is there a signature win you want to focus on? Put it here. Your profile statement should include your primary field, years (but see the cautionary note below) or level of experience, and critical skills or expertise. You can also highlight organizational and leadership strengths from your volunteer experiences in this top section.

Ageism alert: Experts say you may want to avoid putting a number of years when describing your experience in this profile section. Beginning a profile with phrases like "fifteen years experience" in the summary may not be a good idea, especially if the job is calling for five to seven years. Instead say, "extensive experience" or "deep experience."

Ginny's profile:

Communications professional with extensive experience in strategic communications and advocacy on behalf of policy, political, and mission-driven initiatives.

Returner Alicia Schober's profile showcased her unpaid work in the community:

Mission-centric leader, collaborator, critical thinker, skilled communicator, and creative problem solver who is organized, detail oriented, and diligent. Community connector who champions lasting positive change and rallies support for common-good initiatives.

Core Competencies

Core competencies should appear as a bulleted or vertical-bar paragraph just under your professional summary. Also called Skills, Expertise, or Specialties, this section showcases your stable of skills and is an efficient way to speak directly to the requirements in a particular job listing. You will want to use current key words from your industry or the top skills noted in job listing itself. If you are submitting your résumé through an applicant tracking system (ATS), these words will help your résumé get picked up. Big employers use automated systems to weed through résumés before a human ever sees them, and according to ZipRecruiter, these systems reject 80 percent of the résumés within eleven seconds. Having the right words on your résumé will help it get through the robots. For a human reader, seeing a list of core competencies is necessary to know that you have the relevant skills needed for the job. Note that these skills should also appear in the experience section in the context of what you did.

Kerry Strollo has been recruiting for twenty years and sees a lot of résumés. Now a principal recruiter with a top government contractor, Strollo says this list of key words is critical. "List all the different kinds of words that you think will get picked up. It could be the industry, it could be acronyms, technology—it can just be twenty words. List those different types of job titles that you were not in but are equivalent to the role you played. Things you'd be qualified for. You'll get more hits that way."

And, as always, be sure to customize this section for each employer and job.

What's more, don't be afraid to list "soft" skills, some of which you may have been using in your volunteer work. A lot of core team skills never go out of style: managing people, being able to resolve conflict, and having effective sales negotiation and communication skills. Whether you've been out for a week or for a decade, whether you have spent ten years in a field or a career in a different area, many of those core soft skills are more valued than ever and highly transferable.

Ginny pulled hers from her current and past work:

Areas of Expertise
women's 50+ empowerment advocate | author | communications strategy | marketing | media relations | public relations | political

communications | media planning | web content development | interview prep

Returner Alicia Schober again emphasized paid and unpaid work in her list:

SPECIALTIES

project management | community affairs & development | process improvement | idea generation | resource planning | organizational planning | community outreach | strategic partnerships | account management | relationship management | volunteer engagement | volunteer recognition | marketing communications | event planning | teaching & training | presentation skills

Experience

For each role or job, paid or unpaid, you will want to include your employer name, job title, location (city and state), and the dates of employment followed by a description of the job and your responsibilities as well as a bulleted list of accomplishments (not job duties!) at each job. Remember to be consistent in how you format this section.

This bulleted list should be a list of what Fairygodboss president and cofounder Romy Newman calls your "signature wins" in each job or volunteer position. Be strategic about how you choose, describe, and organize them. Make these accomplishments clear, logical, vivid, and compelling. Where possible, use language that mirrors the job description you are applying to—connect the dots between your signature wins and what this job is calling for. Use the PAR method—problem, action, result. What *problem* or opportunity did you work on? What *action* did you take? What skills did you use to fix the problem? What was the *result*? Make these accomplishments stand out, and be sure to quantify them whenever possible—even the unpaid positions.

For example, don't just say you "planned, coordinated, and executed press conferences." Use data. Say you "planned 15 press conferences per quarter to create brand awareness, which resulted in an increase of 15 percent in sales and 150 new press mentions." Framing your accomplishments this way allows you to tell a story and highlight what you excel at.

Our friend Alicia Schober framed one of her community volunteer roles this way on her résumé:

> Parks & Recreation Commission, Designated Alternate Selected by Cupertino City Council: Participated in master planning commission meetings. Proposed all-inclusive playground initiative for the city, established development opportunity with strategic local foundation that resulted in strong support for the park.

The focus on accomplishments, both paid and unpaid, engages the reader, makes you memorable, distinguishes you from others, helps the employer connect the dots, and ensures that you tell your story.

But what if your most recent work experience is not relevant to your job search?

If you are like Ginny and are pursuing a different field, be sure to still talk up your highlights. Include the portion chronologically in the Experience section of your résumé, but keep the content brief, stating the position, the number of years you held that position, and a description of that position, then highlight any transferable skills or responsibilities as well as a brief bullet or two listing significant accomplishments. Although these jobs should never outweigh the content of the jobs you held that are directly relevant to the position or field you are pursuing, your goal is still to show that you are successful at everything you do.

In Ginny's case she could highlight the transferable skills from her eight years in real estate—for example, real estate involves marketing, contract negotiations, client development, and working with clients in high-stress situations—and in her case she'd also developed a blog with original content and created and maintained a website. She should likewise note how much volume she moved each year or any awards she won.

If you have a recent gap in your Experience section and feel you need to explain it, include a brief, honest, and upfront explanation of it. But be sure to keep it short while also letting employers know that you are ready to get back to work. All you need are the dates of your career break with a brief statement: "Took a career break to care for family/kids/parents."

Résumé expert Dowling suggests a statement like this might read something like: "Chose to take a career hiatus to raise my children, during which time I maintained my coding skills through ongoing training and periodic contract assignments. Now that my children are older, I am eager to return to my full-time career."

"Just be upfront and honest, be short and succinct," advises veteran recruiter Strollo. "Don't be funny—don't say you were a 'family engineer.' If you wanted to say that from 2010 to 2012 you cared for a sick parent, that's honorable. Or say you raised your family. But what goes hand in hand with that? Were you a volunteer or productive elsewhere? What did you do to keep your skills alive? Think about how you are spending your time and using your mind."

Extensive Experience

People in their fifties or beyond are sometimes counseled to remove earlier jobs. You may have heard advice like "only include the last ten years of your work"—which, of course, is a problem if you've been on a career break for the last ten years. How do you ensure that your résumé doesn't completely gobsmack the twenty-eight-year-old hiring manager?!

Breathe and own your grown-up value. At this point you've had a lot more experience than that twenty- or thirty-something—and that's good. Your goal is to maximize the more recent and most relevant experience while also acknowledging but not overemphasizing experience that's decades old. One way to do this: under a heading such as "Early Career Progression" just list earlier job titles, companies, and years worked. Gary Burnison, CEO of powerhouse executive search firm Korn Ferry and author of *Lose the Résumé, Land the Job*, told *Next Avenue* that the current and most relevant experience should take up 75 percent of the detail of your professional experience.

You will likely need (at least) a two-page résumé if you have a few decades of work under your belt, and experts say that's okay. If you are twenty-eight, a two-page résumé is probably not right. But if you are in your forties, fifties, or beyond, you've had time to accumulate a few decades of significant work history, multiple degrees and certifications, a strong technical skills inventory, and shelves of industry awards—and you'll need that second page.

"In most cases, a candidate with multiple pages of essential accomplishments can create a two-page résumé and then share secondary information—such as project details, key transaction lists, presentations, publications—in a résumé addendum, which is a separate document. It is worth noting that in academia or scientific fields, a multipage CV is quite common and expected," says Dowling.

Education

Yikes! I graduated during the Reagan years! Should I not list my graduation dates? It is ridiculous to think that an employer won't do the math (if they care) and figure out your graduation dates. Experts say that you don't need to put in your year of graduation if you are concerned about drawing attention to your age. "Showing the degree completion year is common for recent graduates because it helps to explain why a candidate has limited work experience," says Dowling. But for an established candidate with significant work experience, showing the year isn't necessary. The proper listing of the degree is to signify completion, not the year it was completed. In some cases showing a graduation date from the 1970s, 1980s, or even the 1990s can create unintentional bias; instead, just list your college and graduate school institutions and degrees earned.

Other Credentials

These next sections—or variations on them—are a great way to show that you are updated and have relevant skills:

Professional Development. If you have taken classes, workshops, or training or if you have received certifications that are relevant to the job you are seeking, put those here.

Professional Memberships, Affiliations, and Board Memberships. If you serve on the boards of organizations or have relevant professional memberships or affiliations, be sure to list those too.

Technical Skills. If you are in a tech-related field and have the latest skills—such as programming and software skills, like Python—list them. However, do *not* list skills that are either dated or that you are expected to have (i.e., knowledge of PowerPoint).

References? Experts say not to waste space on your résumé by stating the obvious "References available on request" or listing references. If the employer wants references, they will ask.

However, we loved this idea: perhaps include a quote from a reference. Recruiter Kerry Strollo says she loves it when she sees a quote from a reference. "If your manager gave you a reference, pull a quote from it, like 'Sally was miraculous at putting together this fundraising campaign.' Put the quote near the top of your résumé—I love seeing that because it gives you some insight into what another person thinks about the candidate."

Ginny included a quote from a publication that had profiled her work as a Hill press secretary. She included it in the Experience section with that specific job. Using a quote like this is a way of giving your résumé more color and your accomplishments credibility. You can put it at the top as Strollo suggests, put it with the job it references, or add it to your highlights column.

Another approach: rather than call references, these days recruiters and hiring managers are likely to look at the endorsements section of your LinkedIn profile. All the more reason to have your LinkedIn profile powered up (more on that in Chapter 9).

Your Résumé Should Be a Dynamic Document

In the old days people had one résumé. Today you should tweak your résumé for each different job posting you apply to. (Keep your original, and then have different versions of it.) That's important because each job posting can get hundreds of résumés, and if yours doesn't have certain key words, it will not even be considered. So look at the job posting and put it next to your résumé. If what's in the job posting that you are qualified for is not in your résumé, then you need to edit your résumé to work those key words from the job description into your résumé.

For example, if the words "media pitches" or "event planning" or "writing and editing" or "project management" keep coming up in job postings that you are interested in, then you need to make sure your résumé—either in your descriptions of your experiences or in your Core Competencies or both—include those words (while, of course, keeping it honest). Again, you need to connect the dots between your experience and the job description. And know that when recruiters are searching online, they're searching for their key words.

Or take it a step further, advises résumé expert Dowling. Do some research, identify the employer's needs, and then adjust your résumé accordingly. What issues are they facing? What problems are they trying to solve? What projects do they have coming up? Target your message to make the connection between your experience and what they need. Use the profile area of your résumé to call out expertise in a particular project type, product, market, technology, or function.

FlexProfessionals' Sheila Murphy says to always have a "go-to" résumé: "Keep a bank of accomplishments and skills in a separate document, and add and subtract as needed to make yourself most attractive to the target job or company."

If you have multiple career targets, you should customize your résumé for each application. "Create a résumé for each target employer or job type. For example, one career path may be compliance manager at a pharmaceutical firm, and another path may be in government relations. A third could be a position in academia. The skills are similar, but the specific duties and requirements are different," says Dowling. "Create a differentiated message for each target position."

However, don't overdo it. If and when you get to that interview, you will need to own your résumé and be able to speak to it.

Get Feedback

Once you have a draft of your résumé in decent shape, take a deep breath and start sharing it with trusted allies. Have friends or former colleagues review your résumé two ways. First, have them give it the typical six- to twenty-second recruiter scan. What stands out? Does it catch their attention (in a good way)? What are the deficits? Do they think you will get responses, and if not, what can you change to make it better? Do they think the format is appropriate for your field? Maybe that super-cool infographic résumé you took days to put together (the pictures! the graphs! the colors!) is not right for your return to investment banking. (Maybe you need to be in the design field.)

It is really important to get feedback not just so you can make changes but also so you'll have outside perspectives on your résumé. Don't take it personally and melt down, even though you spent weeks putting it together. Everyone you show it to may have different opinions—attagirls and criticisms. Listen to all of them. Maybe you won't incorporate all of their suggestions, but it is good for you to understand that someone else reading it might look at it differently from how you intended the reader to see it. This is the formal feedback that you will need—you are lucky to get it!—on your résumé, your pitch, your LinkedIn profile, your interview practice. Liz Bentley says it comes back to being able to see your truth and where you are on that all-important map right now. "If I look at my résumé, I might think it's fantastic, that this experience I have is so terrific. Someone else's version of that same truth might be that they think that experience is silly, that it doesn't matter, that it's not something that should be highlighted, and, in fact, they think it could even make me look bad. Does that mean I should change my whole résumé? Not necessarily. But I need to not be afraid of difference or of people who see things completely differently from me." This feedback is critical both for the changes you can choose to incorporate from it as well as to give you insight about how your résumé might be received once you launch it.

And proof it well, of course. Ask a friend with a really good eye to comb through it for typos and misspellings. According to research done by Careerbuilder and Adecco, 61 percent of recruiters will reject a résumé on the spot if it contains typos, and 43 percent of hiring managers will disqualify a candidate if the résumé or cover letter has spelling errors.

Targeting your résumé and using the right words makes a difference. Ginny's friend Rebecca had started her own successful business in property management at the Greenbrier Resort's private home development in West Virginia. She started it with one client and then built it over the course of a decade to 110 clients and 399 subcontractors. When her husband took a new job in the DC area, Rebecca sold her business and began a new job search. She put together her résumé, but even after a decade of building and running a successful property management business, her résumé was not getting any bites. It took working with a résumé coach to make her realize that her résumé did not properly frame all that she had accomplished. For example, there was no mention of marketing and project management—things she had done daily in her business. "I did not even get in the door for an interview because I was missing key words and titles," she told Ginny. She also had not expanded her net wide enough—she was not looking for the right type of job because she didn't know all that was out there. That changed when, in the course of her job search, she came across the Domestic Estate Management Association, attended some of their meetings, and realized that could be a logical career move for her. She rewrote her LinkedIn profile and résumé to include key words that truly reflected her skills and experience and made sense for an estate manager. She sent her résumé to a headhunter and got a call immediately. Rebecca now works as the estate manager for a private family—a role that fits her skill set and experience perfectly and one she might never have thought of or found without widening her net and targeting her résumé.

Beyond the Résumé:
The Online or IRL Portfolio

Creatives—people in advertising, web design, graphic design, photography, content development, publishing—*need* a portfolio. But even if you're not an artist or a writer, today you too could strengthen your job candidacy with a portfolio.

"The real purpose is to provide tangible proof of your value in the workplace," says career coach and corporate trainer Chrissy Scivicque of EatYourCareer.com, and there are plenty of ways to do that. "From outlining project descriptions and showcasing work samples to offering up letters of reference and customer reviews, a portfolio can document your professional accomplishments in any way that makes sense for your gig."

You can design your own with sites like Wix, WordPress, Blogspot, Squarespace, or Tumblr. Or you can hire a designer from Upwork or Fiverr to help you put your online portfolio together. It can help you stand out in a crowd.

Think of yourself as a business and your professional portfolio as a marketing brochure for the services you're selling. By showcasing your skills, abilities, and achievements, your portfolio helps your customers (your employers) and prospects (your potential future employers) understand what services you provide and why they are special—and worth the purchase price!

While in a job interview you can pull your portfolio out as proof of your value. You can share your online portfolio with recruiters and talent managers. Your portfolio will go beyond LinkedIn and way beyond a résumé. "Saying 'I planned a fundraising event from beginning to end' is one thing. Showing the event invitation, program, budget, and volunteer guidelines you put together is completely another," says Scivicque.

What should you include in your portfolio? Your résumé or professional bio; letters of recommendation and client feedback, letters, or emails; awards and recognitions; a list of trainings and courses you've completed; and work samples (this can even be video or audio), project outlines or write-ups, and a list of key accomplishments.

Once you're done, put a link to your portfolio on your résumé, include it in your cover letters, and add it to any profiles you've set up on job sites like TheMuse.com or project sites like HoneyBook or Upwork.

And now it's time to get the word out.

8.

THIS IS A CAMPAIGN

How to Network Your Way Back to Work

I find "networking" difficult. I've always struggled with it, and honestly, I've never been to a networking event that wasn't a bit awkward for me. When it feels so transactional, I feel like a jerk. But when it feels natural, you wouldn't believe what can happen.

Take, for example, the other day. I was on (yet another) plane. I never talk to anyone on planes—I just put my head down. But this time I was seated next to a woman, and somehow we just started talking about family. We talked about husbands, about how hers had passed, about how both of our relationships had rough beginnings in similar ways. Then the conversation shifted to our kids—their growing pains and their hard-won successes—and we discovered a few more points of connection. I told her how proud I was of my daughter, who recently graduated from college and was considering law school. It turned out that this woman I connected with on the plane was a judge, who offered to speak with my daughter. Then we talked about me coming to speak to her women's Invest for Success group in Palm Beach and possibly even doing an event there when this book comes out. When we finally parted that day I thought, *Wow, that was so unexpected.* This woman didn't look like a judge (whatever that's supposed to look like!). I was not planning on net-working. I was planning on putting my baseball hat over my head and pretending to be invisible.

But random encounters can add up to something meaningful. My best networking has always been on the road, out in the field of life. I really believe this: great conversations that have to do with other things end up delivering the best contacts.

I also find that women, especially now, have a fervent desire to help other women. When we decide we're going to help, we get kind of pushy, resolute. Women help other women. We don't just say, "Oh yeah, yeah, yeah—call me." The attitude is: "I'm gonna get this done for you." At least, that's the way I am. And that's how women have been for me.

Women are just wired to network and find multiple ways to con-nect and help each other. Audi Melsbakas, who re-entered the finan-cial industry after a nine-year break, says women were critical to her successful job search. At the time she was recently divorced with five children. She started by picking up a part-time position with a small financial adviser, then she did some consulting, then she applied herself in earnest to searching for a full-time job.

She thought about going back to her old company, but that com-pany had shut down their Chicago office. Audi spent a lot of time trying to infiltrate the returnship programs, but she didn't find one in her region. So she started reaching out to her business school con-tacts and former colleagues, the vast majority of whom were men now at the senior level.

She found that very few of her male contacts were willing to help. "They would question: 'Do you really think you can do this? You have five kids? Forget about the idea of traveling,' they would automatically say, 'there's no way you can travel.'" Time and again she felt like the men reflexively doubted her performance level.

She would explain that she was anxious to get back, that her kids are older, that she has an infrastructure of support and a fire in her belly. But still they seemed reluctant to put themselves out there and recommend her. "Most of the men I was speaking to, their spouses were not working. I think they found it really hard to look at me and not think, 'Why would you want to come back to work?'"

She discovered that women were better advocates. One woman in particular, a managing director at a major bank, put her in front of a great number of people. She was the same age and also had kids—she understood. Audi met many women through personal networking who would then introduce her to other women. "The women I was talking to—the vast majority are mothers. They didn't bat an eye. They knew it could be done." She never had to explain to other women why she wanted to come back.

"When I was interviewing at BMO, my two bosses were women with families. I don't think they questioned whether I could balance. They did not question my commitment."

Audi is now a director for BMO Wealth Management US.

Ginny was reminded of the power of women's networks when she started working on this book. What began as a research group—a get-together that Ginny dubbed "Cocktails and Career Conversations"—turned into something unexpectedly moving and motivating.

It was the perfect July evening, and Ginny had gathered a group of fifteen women together to talk about their careers. The women—all friends and all approaching or in their fifties—saw each other during the summer and would usually discuss their now high school– and college-aged children, travel, work, and volunteer commitments. Many of them had known each other for well over a decade. But that night instead Ginny had invited them to reflect on career breaks, pivots, and reinventions.

When Ginny sent out the invitation she was not sure how things would go. Would they think she was crazy? Would they really want to open up about their career histories and hopes? She had no idea what to expect.

The group was a mix of eleven working and four stay-at-home moms. They had some serious educational and career pedigrees. Their career paths were varied: among the attendees were former Fidelity Investment executives, former Fortune 100 executives, an interior designer who had worked for a top New York firm, a scientific researcher with a PhD, a top hair colorist, a human resources director, an occupational therapist, and an artist.

The stories and truths that came tumbling out that evening carried advice and lessons learned from the trenches of working motherhood. They talked about how motherhood had changed the career trajectory for nearly all of them. They talked about reinventions and pivots. Entrepreneurships. Comebacks. And the power of being fifty-something.

Many of their career transitions included launching entrepreneurial ventures—a woman who started a business offering support services to students at her son's boarding school and another who started a curated collection of clothing and jewelry made by women artisans from all corners of the world. By the end of the evening, after hearing each other's career stories, they were exchanging contacts and talking about how they could help each other. What had been planned as a two-hour event as a chance to get insights for this book turned into an unexpectedly passionate, poignant, and incredibly powerful four-hour-long discussion—a near therapy session that then morphed into an impromptu networking event.

The evening ended with everyone going around with an "ask"—a "can anyone connect me with" or "what would you do if." The advice and asks continued online and in person for weeks afterward.

This is where your comeback career search begins—with conversations with friends. *This* is what networking looks like.

Think about starting your own Comeback Careers Conversation Group. The power of women to listen, advise, and help each other was never more evident for Ginny than that night, and it was a game-changer for Ginny. Lessons learned, networks opened, connections made. That, it turns out, is the power of knowing your— and each other's—value.

———

LET'S GET STARTED. Time to rev up your connections. Networking is critical for anyone looking for a job. After all, 80 percent of jobs are found through some type of networking. For someone who has been out of the workforce or is trying to break into a new field, that number is likely even higher.

As soon as you have any idea of the field you'd like to enter or re-enter, think about contacts from past jobs. Who were your mentors? What colleagues or clients really liked you? Make a list. You need to leverage or rebuild your network by seeking introductions. Then have someone help you get your foot in the door, or walk your résumé into the hiring manager's office. Recruiters are not going to come to you; you need to find these people and get to them. And the people who are most likely to recommend you as an employee are the people who already know you as an employee.

If you have twenty hours a week to devote to your job search, 80 percent of that time should be spent networking, not applying to job postings. "Go about your job search like a marketing campaign, and try to raise your visibility with people while you consistently highlight your key strengths and skills," advises career coach Carroll Welch. Set a goal for yourself to do some kind of networking every day. Try emailing three people every morning—people you worked with directly as well as others in the field. Setting targets can help give some structure to your process.

Keep in mind that networking is most effective not when you're reaching out to ask people for a job but when you're getting in touch to reestablish a relationship or offering something that might be of interest or value to them. Once you're in touch, circling back later to ask for an introduction or a job opportunity will feel less transactional.

But don't target just work contacts. Your world is your network. Get the word out—even the person who cuts your hair might know someone. Your dentist. Your dog walker. Think about all the people that each of those people comes in contact with. You'll be pleased to discover that your network is bigger than you think, and you will find that discussions and advice about jobs can happen anywhere—except when you're at home hiding behind your laptop.

It's on you. "The reality is if you have been out of the workforce, you are not going to be on a headhunter's list," says Diane Flynn of ReBoot Accel. She finds that most women she works with find their jobs through a connection, many through working parents at school. While sitting at a baseball game, talking to another mom or dad who works, they tell them their pitch and find a connection that leads to a job.

There are networking opportunities around you every day. Seize them. Networking happens in line at Starbucks, on the playground, at the dog park, at a neighborhood barbeque, at church functions, at the PTA meeting, at your son's hockey game, at book club, at cocktail parties—you get the idea. So whether you're running into an acquaintance at the post office or sitting at a dinner party next to a friend's husband, take the time to be curious about the people in your orbit. "Stand next to somebody and say, 'Tell me what it is you do again?'" says career coach Barrett-Newman. "Then they will ask you, 'What do you do?' And that's your opportunity to say, 'I am looking for an opportunity in X field.' It's a strategic conversation. It's choosing to talk about something that is not about your last vacation or what the kids are doing or the science project." You make progress just by being open and realizing that any interaction you have with somebody is a potential networking opportunity. Conversations can be both strategic *and* genuine. You just choose to talk about something that is not your last vacation, the weather, or what the kids are doing. You make room to talk about yourself and find out about the other person.

Other conversation starters/opportunities (in everyday life rather than networking events):

- What do you do? (obviously)
- How did you get started in that work?
- What do you like best [or least] about what you do?
- What are the biggest challenges your company or organization is facing right now?
- What do you need help with right now?

You will find new connections by going about your daily life, of course, but purposeful outreach to build networks among specific groups will be even more productive. How can you build community among like-minded people and people in a new industry?

Do as Ginny did and propose a Comeback Careers Conversations (and cocktails or coffee) Group. Include a mix of people—those currently working, returners, and pivoters—and have everyone bring someone they know who is interested in a career change. Or, if your network already includes a few people in your target industry, have everyone bring someone else from the industry and host a discussion of recent developments or topics of particular interest. Or, for a less structured event, bring together just a few friends to take a walk and brainstorm ideas and connections with you.

"When you are transitioning back into the workforce, sharing where you are with the people around you and your friend groups is often most helpful," observes Sue Geremia, a human resources consultant and friend from Ginny's Comeback Career Conversations Group. "As soon as you start communicating about the work you want to do, that gets you into real conversations, people begin to take you seriously, and suddenly someone is going to say, 'Oh, I need a little help doing XYZ,' and you've stepped back in."

If you're not comfortable gathering your own group of like-minded women (and men), there are other places to find groups. For instance, check out the coworking spaces and groups that are popping up across the country right now. The success of WeWork—a community of shared beautiful office space with perks like fruit-infused water, craft beer, office supplies, a buzzy vibe, and built-in networking events—has prompted a bunch of other workspace and networking startups, including a new crop focused on women.

The benefits of these coworking spaces to you now, when you're at a job-transitional point in your career, is the networking (okay, and yoga and meditation classes, craft beer, and nicely stocked locker rooms). These places are all about community, and many host events where you can expand your network, be inspired, or learn.

Check out The Wing (New York, DC, LA, San Francisco, Chicago, Boston, Seattle, and more), a workspace that emphasizes community, connections, and learning, with networking opportunities, including happy hours and talks by notable speakers like Hillary Clinton.

And if you are thinking of going out on your own and could benefit from being around other entrepreneurs, check out the women-focused, spa-like coworking space and business accelerator Hera Hub (San Diego, Carlsbad, DC, Phoenix, Atlanta, and coming soon to Seattle, Houston, Irvine). (See the Resources section for a list of other female-focused coworking spaces.)

There are also online networking groups for every industry. Do a Google search, or ask around to find some in or adjacent to your industry. This is where checking out the LinkedIn profiles of people in your prospective industry is especially useful: see what groups they belong to and what kind of resources they offer. Many of the groups have weekly job listings.

For midlife-related online communities for women, we love CoveyClub and NextTribe. Lesley Jane Seymour's CoveyClub offers original content on issues impacting women forty and over, from work to health to relationships, all through a midlife lens. The content is intelligent, not clickbait. Covey offers live, in-person get-togethers and virtual events (a recent one was about what to do if you are worried about getting fired) as well as a podcast called *Reinvent Yourself.*

The two-year-old NextTribe has both an online and offline community. Cofounders Jeannie Ralston and Lori Seekatz say their site's mission is to "offer information and inspiration with a healthy dose of irreverence for women over forty-five to make you feel heard and understood and to connect you with women as smart and cheeky as you are." We love a group whose mantra is "Age Boldly."

We also love the website WeAreAgeist.com and their inspiring profiles of both women and men at fifty and beyond. Ageist hosted their first conference in June of 2019 looking at the economic and social impact of today's (huge and growing) fifty-plus demographic.

And yes, if you have the opportunity, you should try to go to professional networking events in your target industry. It won't be comfortable at first—or maybe *ever*—but it can be beneficial. To be successful at these events you need to be prepared, be present, and show interest in other people's stories and achievements. Put your phone away. Be an engaged listener, and do your homework on the key people at the event. "If you feel alien, unworthy, shy, or nervous in a room full of powerful players, pretend you're there to report a story," says Morra Aarons-Mele, founder of the social impact agency Women Online and author of *Hiding in the Bathroom: An Introvert's Roadmap to Getting Out There (When You'd Rather Stay Home)*. "Ask people lots of questions. Listen actively. Draw them out. Even the most powerful person enjoys telling their own story."

You can crush it at a networking event if you've been doing your research and are making yourself a subject-matter expert in your field instead of trying to make idle chitchat. "It is much more effective to say, 'I'm excited to hear Guru X speak. Did you read her latest article? I thought it was really controversial,'" says iRelaunch's Cohen. "It will also cause the other person to focus more on the substance of what you are saying."

While you're there, be sure to look your best. Wear a great outfit. Get a blowout if you can. Bring a friend or your "conference spouse." Have your networking "wingman" brag for you, advises Cohen.

Sometimes nerves do take over. When Ginny was at one of my Know Your Value conferences she had the opportunity to meet Senator Kamala Harris. Ginny is a huge fan of Senator Harris and told her that she hoped she would run for president. When Senator Harris asked Ginny why, Ginny says that she froze like a deer in headlights. Later on, after Senator Harris left the room, of course, Ginny thought of about a hundred intelligent things to say, but in the moment she was too starstruck to think straight. Had she known that she would have the chance to meet Senator Harris, she might have been better prepared. The lesson? Practice some talking points in advance in case you get star struck when you run into the CEO of the company you'd like to work for or, say, a presidential candidate you admire. Prepare even for the unexpected at these events.

Making the Connection

The goal of all your networking, obviously, is to find a contact who can offer insight, an introduction, or a personal recommendation to someone at one of your targeted companies. Where does your network overlap with the companies that interest you?

Sometimes you need to be resourceful to find a match between your network and your target. Ginny's friend Laurel knew about a job posting at a company that interested her and noticed that a mom at her daughter's preschool had an email address at that company. She set up a coffee with the other mom and came armed with talking points of how she could do the job based on what she had done in her previous jobs. Based on that encounter Laurel got an interview.

Even if you don't have a first-degree contact leading to the job or company you want, don't give up. You probably know someone who knows someone. But you'll never know unless you ask.

The best help in job searching often comes from your second-degree contacts—the friends, relatives, and contacts of your first-degree network. Go wide, and ask your network for assistance by providing introductions to contacts in your targeted industry. That's what Donna did after being abroad as a trailing spouse for several years. She reached out to former colleagues, sending an email that explained what she'd been doing (in another country with her family), outlined her experience (policy, healthcare, and tech), and said she was looking for work in the United States. She was specific about the kind of role she was looking for and which organizations interested her. She attached her résumé and asked friends and former colleagues to take a look and pass it along. She even mentioned a few names of people she'd like to get in front of. One thing led to another, and she eventually found a job match.

Best Practices for Your Outreach

Reach Out on Email

When you start reaching out to contacts, you'll find people are surprisingly willing to help out. But you can make their job easier—and get better results—if you (concisely!) give them all the information they'll need to hook you up.

As you compose your emails make sure you're sending something your contact can easily forward to someone else. In other words, your message should be clear about who you are, what you can offer, and what you want. Simply explain why you're reaching out; include an overview of your qualifications; a short list of types of positions or companies, associations, or nonprofits that interest you; and include your LinkedIn URL or attach a résumé.

Most importantly: be specific in the email about what you are asking for: Job leads? Informational interviews? Introductions? "Interestingly, the more specific you are, it's often easier for people to connect you with opportunities," Cavoulacos of The Muse told Ginny. And, as always, thank them in advance.

Ask for and Have an Informational Interview

In most cases the networking you do will not connect you to someone who has the perfect job opening at that very moment. Your goal is to get in front of people who work at your company of interest and to be top of mind when a position opens up. Or—best-case scenario—that they like you so much they create a job for you!

This is where the informational interview is so important. The meeting should cost your contact minimal time and the benefit to you is enormous: you will make a connection; get an insider

SUGGESTED COMEBACK CAREER
EMAIL TEMPLATE

Open with a little about your connection to the person: "I hope all is well with you. I have been following your updates on LinkedIn, and it looks like things are great at work!"

Then dive into the purpose of your email: "I am looking to pivot/get back into [specific job/industry]."

Provide some background: "Given my background in [industry/job], I am most interested in [specific job]. I would also be delighted for any opportunity [suggest other possibilities here]. I believe my well-honed [fill in appropriate] skills would also make me a good fit for [add other jobs here]."

Then go for your ask: "I would be most grateful if you would let me know of anything that might be an interesting fit or if you know of anyone who you think would be a good person for me to speak with."

Or if this person is in that field and you are looking for an informational interview: "Would you have some time to tell me a bit more about the latest trends in [your targeted] industry?"

Then let them know that you are including your information for them: "I have attached my résumé and a link to my LinkedIn profile as well."

Close in a professional way: "Thank you. I look forward to staying in touch."

perspective on the industry, company goals, and applicant requirements; possibly get referrals to other contacts; and maybe even land their personal recommendation when the time comes.

If you find a connection in your network who is in an industry or with a company of interest, reach out to that person and ask if they have time for a phone call or, better, if they will have coffee with you. Don't ask them for a job, because then they may say they don't know of any, and then your conversation is over. Instead, say you are pivoting/returning to work and considering X industry/field and would like to get their insights.

When you meet with this person, be prepared. Look at their LinkedIn profile. Research the company/industry. Be familiar with industry lingo. Do enough research that you know who the biggest players are and be able to talk about the most important trends. This is a chance for you to make a good impression and come across as credible and serious. Open the conversation by thanking them for their time, reminding them who connected you, and giving them a quick thumbnail of your background and what you are looking for. Don't get into a long pitch, but do let this person know what your goals are so they understand how they can help you. If you are focused on a specific job or company, let them know.

Then start asking questions. It's fine to have them written down (you look prepared!) and excellent to take notes (you look serious!). Below are some questions to ask. Of course, you should tailor them to your situation, but the point is to use this time to find out whether this company/industry/organization has jobs or roles that match your skills and background and to figure out what that company/industry/organization is looking for.

Here are some basic questions when you are trying to learn about a company or role:

- How did you get your start in this field?
- What's the most rewarding part of your job/field?
- What do you not like about it?
- What's changing in this field?
- What are your biggest challenges right now?
- What kinds of people do well in this industry?
- What are the worst parts of your job?

- What didn't you know before you got into this industry that you wish someone had told you?

If you are still exploring different career paths and want to find out if a pivot to this area is right for you, you could ask:

- How did you choose this company or position over others in your field?
- My background is in [fill in the blank here]. How do you think I can best leverage my previous experience for this field?

If you're further along in your job search and need some specific advice on your search, ask:

- What job-search advice would you give to someone in my situation?
- What advice can you give me about how to best prepare for an interview with this company/industry?
- What experiences, skills, or personality traits does your company look for in new hires?
- What do you wish you had done differently when you first started at your company?
- Based on what you know about my background, what do you see as my weaknesses?
- What would I need to do to offset a hiring manager's potential concerns about my career gap/pivot/age?

These are key questions for you to ask, and they can help you suss out where you may need to upskill or how much of an issue your career break/pivot/age could be.

Is this the time to ask about money? Sure, but be careful. Don't ask the person how much they make, but you can say you've done some research, and it seems that $XX,000 to $XX,000 is the typical salary range for the X position, then ask if this sounds accurate.

The Don'ts

Don't use this time to ask this new contact to put in a good word for you for a position. That immediately makes things uncomfortable. However, if a position opens up at their company and you are applying for it, it is okay to follow up and let them know that you are applying for the job. Let them volunteer whether they want to vouch for you.

Don't take a huge amount of their time. If in your request you said a twenty-minute coffee, keep it to twenty minutes. If the conversation is going well and you are about at the twenty-minute mark, politely ask if they have time to continue.

Don't give up if you get negative feedback. This person might tell you that you're not qualified, you are too old, you're out of the loop, and so on. Remember: this is one person's opinion. Don't give up! If you are really interested, talk to other people in the company/industry.

Don't forget to end any conversation with a good contact by asking, "Do you know if there is anyone else I could speak to?"

Following up now and later is key. Always, always, always follow up with a thank-you email within twenty-four hours and even a handwritten note. Keep in mind that the real purpose of informational interviews is not just to find out information but also to build relationships and allies who will champion you in the future. This meeting has the potential to be so much more than twenty minutes in a coffee shop. Figure out ways to keep in touch, not in an annoying way but in a way that is helpful and shows you were listening to the person's advice. Refer to something you learned in the conversation, say you read the book she suggested and here's what you thought of it/learned, forward an article they might find interesting.

Keep them updated on your job search and let them know about any meetings you have with contacts they recommended. This person is now part of your network and can be a helpful ally in the future if you handle this right.

Networking on Social Media

LinkedIn

LinkedIn is the perfect place for online networking because it was created for that purpose. LinkedIn has more than six hundred million members. We'll go into more detail about how to use LinkedIn in a later chapter, but as a networking tool it's ideal. So much information about potential contacts is available. You can not only search for people at a particular company or with a specific job title, but you can also see whether you have alumni or other connections in common. You can see how people who work in your target industry present themselves, what kind of experience they have, what groups they've joined, and more. All of this detail helps you find more points of connection and more ways to focus your approach.

Ginny found LinkedIn to be a huge resource while working on this book as well as in her job search. As she built her connections, her newsfeed became an invaluable source of information and contacts. By getting involved in conversations on the site and publishing articles she'd written, she was able to build her own profile and visibility in the area of career transitions.

Once your LinkedIn profile is updated and polished (see Chapter 9), you can start connecting with people and begin building your LinkedIn community. According to LinkedIn, 35 percent of the users say that a casual conversation on the network has led to a new opportunity. Nearly two-thirds—61 percent—of LinkedIn users found that regular online interaction with their professional network can lead to possible job opportunities.

If you have just lost your job, get on LinkedIn immediately and update your profile, set up job alerts, connect with colleagues and friends, and monitor your feed regularly.

"LinkedIn is a gift to relaunchers," says iRelaunch's Cohen. The same can be said for anyone looking for a job. Don't be afraid to reach out to those long-lost people from your working past. If you think they won't remember you or won't respond because you haven't been in touch for ten years, reach out anyway. It's a no-lose situation. If they don't respond, you are in the same place you are in now. If they do respond, you are well ahead.

Here's a sample script of what you could say:

Dear Christina,

Thanks for connecting with me on LinkedIn! It has been a long time, and it is great to be back in touch. I'm returning to work after a ten-year career break/pivoting to a new industry, and I'm exploring options right now and assessing where I can add value. One field/job/company/industry I'm looking into is X. Who do you recommend I follow or what websites do you think I should keep up with that will help me get up to date in the field? I value your opinion greatly and appreciate any suggestions you may have.

Figure out who in your network either works at or is connected with an employee at your targeted employer, then reach out to them by email to request an introduction or conversation. Do this regardless of whether a job opening exists! By establishing contacts within your company of interest, you can learn about opportunities before they are posted and make inroads into positions before other candidates can.

Once you build your LinkedIn network, start flipping through your LinkedIn newsfeed every day. Your newsfeed is a hugely valuable resource. You learn the lingo and identify and follow thought leaders in the field. You'll become familiar with issues and conversations happening in the field, giving you the opportunity to engage in conversations and connect with others. You can reinforce your professional brand by finding, sharing, and commenting on the content in your feed as well as sharing it through other social media sites like Twitter, Facebook, or Instagram. You also can create, develop, and amplify your own voice in your chosen field or industry. LinkedIn is an amazing resource in your professional comeback.

Facebook

If you are active on Facebook, this is a good place to let people know that you are transitioning, but remember that posts here are typically more personal—vacation photos, funny dog videos, and the like—so keep it light. Try posting that you are excited about heading in a new direction, and then share what you are doing.

Here is a sample post:

> Excited to share with my #FBFriends that I am charting a new course and will be re-entering the world of public relations. Looking for work at a nonprofit. You've always had my back with the best contractor and Thai-takeout suggestions—I'd love your advice on my job search. Here's a link to my updated LinkedIn profile!

If you've just lost your job, there is no shame in asking for help. You may not want to blast "I just got laid off" with an obscene GIF from *The Office* (although it would stand out among all the baby animal videos and lovely family vacation pics). But you might post something like:

> Going through a job transition and would love some help from my #FBFriends. Looking for opportunities in or adjacent to the advertising world, where I've been an account executive for two decades. My top accounts have included airlines and the travel industry. If you have advice or someone to connect me to, I'd be grateful. Here's a link to my updated LinkedIn profile and my online portfolio.

———

REMEMBER: networking does not have to feel inauthentic. Think about what you can give back. How can you be a resource to someone so that the relationship is beneficial to both of you? Offer to connect people or give a shout-out on social media to someone, offer your skills to help someone in your network, send someone an article to let them know you are thinking of them. Networking is about building relationships.

At this point you have a good idea of how to start expanding your network—you're dusting off old connections, acknowledging recent ones, reaching out for new ones. With any luck you're starting to feel some momentum. There's just one more thing you need to do before (re)launching yourself into your next and best career: make sure your online presence is as put together as the rest of you.

9.

STOP FEARING LINKEDIN AND MASTER YOUR DIGITAL TOOLKIT

When Ginny first started working with the Know Your Value team she began reaching out to thought leaders and experts, requesting interviews for her book research. But her LinkedIn profile for the first couple of months still said that she was a realtor. Her realtor website came up. Her early attempts at tweeting dating back to the 2012 presidential race came up. People were confused! Ginny's digital footprint was a hot mess. She thought she had updated the profile when she threw in some language about joining Know Your Value. Oops.

The first thing anyone should do before beginning a job search or trying to establish themselves in a new career is to take care of deferred maintenance on your digital footprint. Build your new digital footprint on LinkedIn and other social media with a strategy: know your goal, and know who you are trying to reach. This needs to be more than filling in the blanks and engaging in some haphazard social media engagement.

What message do you want to send when a potential employer—or anyone, for that matter—Googles you? Your likes, tweets, and shares as well as your LinkedIn profile can be a huge asset in rebooting your professional brand—or they can sink you. Even if you are just reaching out for an informational interview, make sure you've established an online presence or at least make sure yours isn't a mess (like Ginny's was). Even having no LinkedIn profile can raise a red flag and make people wonder if you are technologically unsavvy or if you're out of it or dated.

I am very active on social media—I tweet about three times a day, and I post to Instagram at least once a week, usually more. Anyone in the media today has to be active on social media. I have separate personal accounts and business accounts, of course, but they have one thing in common: I'm always sharing things that people might connect with on a personal level. I use social media to amplify my *Morning Joe* and Know Your Value brands to carry on a constant dialogue with my *Morning Joe* audience and to inspire and teach my Know Your Value audience.

You might not need a social media following, but you *do* need a social media footprint that aligns with your professional brand. For most people this starts with LinkedIn. But depending on the industry you are targeting, different kinds of social media may have different levels of importance for you. "If you are looking to relaunch as a teacher, Twitter may be less helpful than if you are relaunching in tech or advertising, where regular tweeting may be expected," says career coach Carroll Welch. "If you want to relaunch as a landscape designer or graphic artist—those are visual fields, and Instagram (or Pinterest) will be more helpful than LinkedIn. Know your industry and which social media platforms will be most helpful."

Social media like LinkedIn gives you a great opportunity to strategically build and shape your new professional brand and message. Get excited—it's time to make friends with social media.

Clean Up the Digital You

As Ginny learned, you might need to do a little housekeeping. Go ahead and Google yourself (as any potential employer might), and see what comes up. You've left digital breadcrumbs through all your social media channels. What do they say about you? Even if it's not bad stuff, just to have mixed messages or no footprint is, at best, a wasted opportunity and, at worst, detrimental to your progress.

Only about half of LinkedIn's six hundred million members are active monthly. Like Ginny, many are not tending their profiles. They open an account, fill out a few fields, and forget about it. Ginny's was a case of benign neglect—she had set up a profile years before and thought she had updated it, but it was a confusing mess.

Employers research candidates online to gauge their professionalism, to evaluate their possible fit into their company culture, and to learn more about their qualifications. It's okay to show hobbies and family on your social media; things like that round you out. But avoid controversial messages, too much cutesy stuff, and oversharing, and definitely keep it clean. You want to stay consistent with your professional brand message and create a new digital footprint. The best way to do that is to create or refresh your LinkedIn profile, and then get active on LinkedIn and other appropriate social media.

Get (Back or Refreshed) on LinkedIn

LinkedIn is going to be your best friend as you go about your professional reboot. This is where the brainstorming you've already done for your pitch, your personal brand value, and the core competencies you isolated on your résumé come into play. Keep in mind that potential employers are likely to review your résumé *and* your LinkedIn profile, so there's value in making them complementary.

But don't make the mistake of thinking that LinkedIn is just a place where your résumé lives online. For Pete's sake, don't cut and paste your new résumé into your LinkedIn! (Yes, that's exactly what Ginny did when she set up her profile a few years ago.) You would be missing a huge opportunity.

Unlike your bulleted, one- to two-page, black-and-white e-doc résumé, LinkedIn gives you the chance to present a full 360-degree view of who you are and what you've done. You can make it come alive and captivate your audience and potential employers by expanding on your résumé bullets and really telling stories about your accomplishments. You can use a more conversational tone in your profile, summary, and descriptions. Your copy can be more engaging and really show your personality, personal philosophy, and values. Unlike your résumé, you can give the backstory—tell why you love what you do or even how you got started in it. On LinkedIn you can make your accomplishments come alive by adding media-rich entries—like videos, published articles, and links—that showcase your accomplishments. And you can add the words of others: you can prove your value by including showstopper recommendations and endorsements from former colleagues and bosses. Then, once you've rebooted your profile, you can engage with others in your field—sharing articles, commenting on their posts, even publishing your own articles—and really start solidifying your new professional brand.

Unlike your résumé, however, you won't tailor your LinkedIn profile to each job application. Although it will look different when you are looking for a job versus when you are not looking (more on that later), and you will still want to update it on a regular basis, you'll only have one LinkedIn profile.

There are a few key components of a LinkedIn page—the headline, summary, experience, and skills—as well as lots of fun features that make it so much more multidimensional than your résumé. We

---

NOTE

Remember: when you are updating your profile, make sure to adjust the privacy settings to prevent your network from being notified each time you make a change. Here's how:

Click the Me icon at the top of your LinkedIn homepage.

Select Settings & Privacy from the dropdown.

Click the Privacy tab at the top of the page.

Under the How Others See Your LinkedIn Activity section, click Change next to Share Job Changes, Education Changes, And Work Anniversaries from Profile.

Switch the toggle to No.

---

asked career communications coach Katie Fogarty, whose company The Reboot Group works with clients and companies to tell better career and brand stories, to give us her best advice and help Ginny and Laura with their LinkedIn profiles.

Ready? Let's get started!

Start with a Great Headline

It sounds basic, but you need to start with a strong headline that tells what you do. The headline is the most prominent part on your LinkedIn profile, and it needs to serve as a "quick and powerful elevator pitch," says Fogarty. It is limited to 120 characters and should include key words that share your expertise and what you have to offer. These 120 characters are your personal brand story in fewer characters than the old Twitter format. People will look for you on

LinkedIn because either they already know your name or because they are searching for someone with your expertise. So utilize those keywords: your name and what you offer should appear in the headline. For formatting we like the vertical bar with a space on either side between the keywords or phrases to give the information a clean, professional look.

For example, a terrific headline for someone who worked in lobbying and has an MBA is:

Government Relations & Business Operations | Strong Analytic, Writing & Management Ability | MBA

Or, for someone who worked in the executive suite, a strong headline could be something like:

C-Level Operations & Management Support

You can always just keep it simple and add "pro" or "experienced" to your title, depending on your experience. For example, "Experienced Sales Leader," "Financial Services Pro," and "Experienced Content Developer" are all headlines that jump off the page.

Before Ginny started redoing her profile, her headline said "Realtor," which, for starters, was no longer accurate. Her headline needed to say what Ginny was working on now (a contributor and developer of original content for Know Your Value). Because she was looking to get back into the communications field, she also included her previous job title from Capitol Hill. And because she was no longer pursuing a real estate career, it made no sense to have "Realtor" in the headline at all. Also note that her maiden name is included so that people who knew her before she married Ian could find her. This is helpful as well if you have a more common last name like Smith or Jones.

Ginny (Flynn) Brzezinski
Know Your Value, Comeback Careers | Contributor | Original
Content | Former Capitol Hill Press Secretary

Let Your Summary Tell Your Story

The Summary section should be a profile that tells your professional story and defines your personal brand. It should let viewers know what sets you apart, what your "secret sauce" is. If you are job hunting, it should focus on your past work and skills. If you are currently employed, it should focus on what you do now.

While similar to the profile on your résumé, the LinkedIn summary can be more conversational than the profile at the top of your résumé. You've got more space—two thousand characters! Having said that, the first two lines need to capture your audience and encapsulate your value proposition directly and quickly, as they are the only lines that will be seen without clicking through the drop-down. Go ahead and tell your story in first person.

Here is Ginny's. The italicized section is what shows before the viewer clicks on the drop-down. Ginny's is written as a narrative, focusing on her current work with Know Your Value. This summary is geared toward defining Ginny and her work for anyone who Googles her. It is not a job-hunting summary. The summary evolved as Ginny's work with Know Your Value evolved and then again when Ginny began actively job hunting.

Here is Ginny's first Summary:

Returning to work after a career break shouldn't be an uphill battle. Which is why I've teamed with my sister-in-law Mika Brzezinski and her Know Your Value team to launch Comeback Careers, *the newest evolution in Mika's nationwide Know Your Value move-ment to empower women in the workplace.*

We're creating a suite of multiplatform content that gives women a roadmap for getting back to work. We'll be sharing proven return-to-work strategies and tools through web content, video, conferences, and events. We're also coauthoring a book about our divergent career arcs and returning to work, coming in January 2020.

I know the return-to-work struggle intimately. I stepped back from a twelve-year Capitol Hill press career when my kids were born. Mika never stopped working. Now, after a career pause and pivot, I am finding my own path back and, in the process, helping others discover theirs. Together, Mika and I are committed to creating a path forward for all women looking for a career return. We know your value. Time to share it with the world.

Here is how it evolved when Ginny began searching for a job:

15+ years of experience in strategic communications and advocacy for policy- and mission-driven initiatives that improve the economic health and lives of working Americans.

Today my mission is empowering women. Along those lines, I'm writing a book with my sister-in-law Mika Brzezinski called *Comeback Careers*, part of the *New York Times* best-selling Know Your Value series. This latest edition focuses on women rein-venting, rebooting, and pivoting careers at midlife (due from Hachette Books in January 2020).

I also create branded content for the NBC News Digital website KnowYourValue.com, writing about women at the in-tersection of life and work. Through my work for the book and website, I've interviewed celebrities, CEOs, members of Congress, and everyday women and told their stories in print, digital, and on video. I'm inspired by every one of them.

I spent 12 years as a Capitol Hill press secretary for a senator and for two major Senate committees, working on issues from taxes, healthcare, and trade policy to blockbuster government investigations. Now more than ever, I remain passionate about politics and policy.

But what do I focus on in my Summary if I have not worked for a few years . . . or decades?

Just like with your résumé, you'll need to identify your value to current employers by thinking about what in your past work history—and current life—makes you marketable today. This is a combination of the expertise you built in your past work life and the steps you've taken more recently to remain current, such as continuing education, volunteer work, and any new interests that fuel your pivot or return. Get a grip on the current lingo—print out a few job descriptions that interest you and study them: What are the key words that these organizations are using to describe this position? What is the title? What are the soft skills? Then start going through your professional and volunteer experiences and apply that vocabulary. Always keep your goal and audience in mind. If you have been a full-time parent and out of the workforce for more than a few years, acknowledge this gap and identify how current activities— whether volunteer work, child rearing, or part-time work—fit into the bigger picture. As with your résumé, you are reclaiming your professional self and reimagining where you can go next.

Remember my best friend, Laura? Laura focused on her work in the energy industry before her career break because that was the industry she wanted to return to. Laura's headline showcased her value proposition—including her energy, business, and government-relations background:

Energy & Environment | Government Relations | Clean Energy Policy | Domestic & International Business Development

Laura's summary also focused on her work—even though it was more than a decade old:

My career snapshot: 10+ years as a government-relations and business-development executive for a global Fortune 500 electric and gas utility. Known for building strong partnerships with federal and state government agencies to advance business goals, delivering actionable business intelligence, and working seamlessly with C-level executives and senior stakeholders. My specialties: energy & environment, federal and state legislative/regulatory work, international business development (Latin America/Europe), sustainable investing, energy finance, project management (operations, data analysis, metrics, reporting), and C-suite/board of directors management and support.

Laura addressed her career gap in this manner:

Most recently I have been on an extended family-care sabbatical, raising a daughter while caring for out-of-state sick parents. With my daughter entering high school and my parents' health challenges resolved, I am returning to work.

Laura says that although her profile did not necessarily bring her a job offer, it showcased her value when someone Googled her by focusing on her experience, not her years out of the workforce.

Punch Up Your Profile!

And here's where things can really get interesting on LinkedIn. Unlike your résumé, you can make yourself and your profile stand out by adding "rich media" to punch up your profile. Have you given a talk or been on a panel? If you have video of it, add it. You can share things like news clips, video clips, interviews, and photos to back up all of your claims of accomplishments.

It's easy: you just add links to rich media at the bottom of the summary. Ginny added links to some of her articles that had appeared on the Know Your Value website. (And she notes that if she can do it, you can too!) Thumbnail photos from each of the articles show up, dressing up your LinkedIn page even more.

Tout Your Experience

The Experience section is where you have the kind of content that appears on your traditional résumé. However, on LinkedIn you can make it come alive. (Again, do not cut and paste your résumé here.) You want to craft Experience blocks that capture a recruiter's eye, so, like your résumé, you will want to use keywords to improve your search engine optimization (SEO). But here you can also humanize the language and make it more conversational than your résumé. Note that LinkedIn features only about four lines of any job description—viewers need to click through to see the rest—but this is still more than you would put on a résumé. Keep in mind, however, that many people won't take the time to click through and read long descriptions. "Keep your job descriptions to between one and three tightly written summary sentences and, for much older roles, no descriptors at all," advises Fogarty.

And you can add media here as well! So drop in links to articles, photos of you speaking at a conference, or video of a presentation you have given. Ginny added links to more articles and video interviews she'd done under her entry for Know Your Value. She added a jpeg of the book jacket under her coauthor entry.

Get a High-Quality, Professional Photo

This is really important. It is not about vanity; it is about your brand. Remember: this is the image that will come up when an employer Googles you. Make it count. No selfies, and no blurry, cutesy, or old photos. Take a look at some LinkedIn profile photos, and see the difference a great photo makes. Maybe you have a friend who knows what they are doing and can take a good photo with a good camera (iPhone X portrait mode is excellent) against a background like a brick wall or trees. If that doesn't work, then book a professional headshot. Keep in mind that this is an investment, so if you don't know anyone, ask your Facebook friends who they recommend. Ginny asked her realtor friends, as they get headshots done regularly. And for the shoot, be sure to dress for the job you want; even get a blowout and consider getting your makeup done professionally for it. It sounds superficial, but appearances matter. And if you are worried about looking old? We love ReBoot Accel's Beth Kawasaki's wisdom: "We don't have to read young, but we have to read current. The two things that ding people first are hairstyle and glasses. Ask yourself: Is there something I can do to update [my image]?" Haircut? New updated glasses frames? Again, this isn't vanity, just reality. Once you get that great photo, use it across all of your social media for consistency when you are Googled.

And don't forget about the cover image. That's the rectangular image behind your headshot. LinkedIn has a generic default image. If there is another image that better supports your branding, use it. This is different from Facebook—for example, Ginny's background image on Facebook is a photo she took of a whale. That may be fine for Facebook, but it's not a good choice for her new professional brand on LinkedIn unless she is applying for a job as a wildlife photographer. Instead, for LinkedIn she used a photo of the stage setting from one of my Know Your Value conferences. Diane Flynn, cofounder of ReBoot Accel, has a background photo of her leading a workshop. Carol Fishman Cohen has a background photo of the iRelaunch logo. Career coach Carroll Welch uses one of the LinkedIn photos of a desk with a laptop. Check out CANVA.com for presized templates so you can easily personalize your own cover image art.

Also, if you haven't already, consider customizing your LinkedIn URL address. At the top-right corner of your LinkedIn profile there's an option to "Edit public profile & URL." Click on it, and you'll see how easy it is to change your LinkedIn address from the randomly assigned address to one that makes sense for your brand, such as *www.linkedin.com/in/jane-doe-communications-specialist.*

Get Connected

As we've already mentioned in Chapter 8, once your profile is refreshed and ready to go, start connecting with people. Connecting through LinkedIn is a great way to reach out to former colleagues and let them know you are looking for a job. Be sure to go beyond clicking on connect—personalize your connection requests. And be selective: try to connect with people who are in your field or have some connection to your field. This helps your news feed focus on issues that are relevant to you.

However, you do want as many connections as you can get. Kawasaki says when a recruiter has fifty candidates, and forty-nine have 500 connections and one has 200, that's a flag. LinkedIn has a 500-connections metric—for example, when you have more than 500 connections, your connections are noted simply as "500+." So if you can get to 500 connections, it's one less thing to discredit you. Kawasaki says she tries to get her clients to at least 250 connections.

Add Skills and Endorsements

A robust Skills section is critical to being discovered on LinkedIn by recruiters and hiring managers, industry leaders, and your network. As with the Core Competencies section of your résumé, Skills should be keyword-rich so it can boost search metrics. LinkedIn allows for up to fifty skills, so make sure your competencies are represented. But don't be random about this. "Make sure the first three listed, which are the only three immediately visible in the current LinkedIn User Interface, are your strongest assets—the skills you are known for today," advises Fogarty.

Unlike your résumé's Core Competencies section, the LinkedIn Skills section lets you show proof of those skills by publishing endorsements from connections. You get these endorsements by asking former colleagues, employers, or friends for testimonials. Be strategic about this: source your recommendations so you wind up with a mix of clients, employers, and colleagues who will endorse you for a variety of specific skill sets. Fogarty recommends using the top three skills in your Skills section as the blueprint for your endorsement strategy. What's more, be creative about your recommendations—they don't all need to be supervisors. Direct reports, colleagues, fellow volunteers, and industry peers can all help provide a 360-degree picture, she advises. Be direct and candid in your request, letting them know that you are finally getting around to updating your profile. Make their job easy by including in your ask the phrases you want discussed in testimonials.

For example: *Dear James: Would you be willing to write a LinkedIn recommendation about my ability to do XYZ?* Or: *Dear Anna: Thanks for agreeing to be a LinkedIn recommender. Would you consider focusing your remarks on my work to do ABC?*

If you are pivoting and want to earn credibility for skills that aren't currently featured on your profile, you can click the "Add a skill" link and request endorsements for that particular expertise. Some people will put off asking for endorsements because it feels uncomfortable, but we've heard that recruiters and hiring managers are taking these very seriously—after all, it's easier to check your LinkedIn endorsements than to call your references. So if you have useful contacts who are enthusiastic about you, by all means, ask them to say so online!

And be sure to get as many recommendations as you can—one or two is not enough. LinkedIn requires at least *three* recommendations for your profile to be considered "complete," which then boosts SEO and makes your profile more discoverable.

Add Certifications and Courses

Add any certifications or courses you've taken that can make you more marketable. This is especially important if you are returning after a career break or pivoting. Adding Certifications and/or Courses sections can show that you've kept your skills up or that you are serious about refreshing dated skills to be more marketable. If you are working on a certification, you can add a line that says, "Anticipated [fill in the blank] certification, fall 2020." When the certification is complete, this line can be changed to reflect the updated status. (See the Resources section for a list of online learning resources with classes that can be completed in a weekend or a few weeks.)

Publish, Like, Comment, and Share

And now it's time to really engage by publishing your own articles or commenting on and sharing other people's posts and articles. Although publishing original content will give you the most visibility (only one million of the six hundred million LinkedIn users have published their own articles), if you are not ready to do that, you can start by liking and commenting on other people's articles and posts. This puts you in the conversation and encourages others to engage with you. It also builds a track record of likes, shares, and comments that reinforce your brand. Post regularly—at least twice a month—to keep your connections' attention and rise to the attention of others in your field.

Beth Kawasaki of ReBoot Accel says the rule of thumb is: "If you are in an active job search, be on LinkedIn in the morning and at night. If you are not in an active job search, it is great to engage once a day. Don't do the same thing every day. Like something one day. Add a quality comment and share a post another day. Then bring in an article, and really take some time to craft what you are going to say about it."

Your engagement is tracked, categorized, and posted "above the fold" in the Articles and Activity section—and here's why that matters. "If you are trying to move ahead in your career or business, you want viewers to see that you are a regular and quality contributor," says Kawasaki.

Kawasaki explains the five levels of engagement on LinkedIn and advises mixing it up:

Like. Indicates you've read and positively responded to the headline and some or all of the content of someone else's post.

Comment. You've read and thought about someone else's post and contributed your expertise and perspective to the conversation.

Share. You've liked and commented, and now you think this post would be valuable to your connections, so you share it with them, adding a substantive comment about why you're sharing it.

Post. You've discovered—and read thoroughly—an article elsewhere and want to share it with your connections by posting it to your timeline along with a value-add comment to help start a conversation on LinkedIn.

Publish. You've authored an article of original content reflecting your expertise and unique perspective on a particular subject. This is the highest form of engagement and contribution, and it requires the most amount of effort. If it gets traction, you've reached the holy grail in personal branding on LinkedIn. Congrats!

"LinkedIn is a community, and the most valuable members are the ones who contribute, connect, and lend support to one another. Be intentional about it," advises Kawasaki. "If you really are trying to create a brand, you should be sharing, commenting, posting, or bringing in articles and possibly publishing content that is contributing to a specific conversation where you are beginning to establish yourself as a subject expert and, potentially, a thought leader."

Update Regularly

Commit to updating your profile quarterly, says Fogarty. Put reminders in your calendar if you have to. "Your profile shouldn't be static. By reviewing it quarterly you can keep it current and continually align it with best practices and career updates." As your career evolves, so too should your LinkedIn.

Beyond LinkedIn—
Twitter, Instagram, and Facebook Groups

When it comes to your job search beyond LinkedIn, other social media platforms can be hugely helpful in establishing credibility, reinforcing your brand, and building your network. But you don't need to be on all of them. Explore the different platforms to see which make sense for you. I use Instagram and Twitter constantly and, to a lesser extent, Facebook as social platforms for *Morning Joe* and Know Your Value. Companies use these sites to communicate with consumers and employees as well as to recruit talent.

Test the waters by opening an account on Instagram or Twitter and then following thought leaders in your field. Then check out who those people are following. Watch the discussion threads. If you are interested in a specific company, follow its Twitter feed or Facebook page. This makes you more conversant in the field and helps you signal to anyone who Googles you that you are following things in the industry and that you are current in social media. If done correctly, your social media can reinforce your résumé and LinkedIn profile.

Once Ginny started writing essays for the Know Your Value website, she would then post them on her social media platforms—Twitter, Instagram, Facebook, and LinkedIn. This all contributed to establishing her voice and building credibility for her.

Twitter is a cinch—you don't even need to tweet. You pick people or companies in your industry to follow, and you can simply like or retweet what they say. When you retweet, you can also comment on their tweet if you like. Building a track record of this will reinforce your brand and is a way of showing you are current.

"If you meet someone who works at that company at an event, or, ideally, if you are in an interview, you should say, 'I was looking at [name of company's] main Twitter page, and I saw the post on X. I clicked through and read it, and this is what I thought, . . .'" advises iRelaunch's Cohen. "This is signaling two things. One, that you are comfortable with social media—'I was looking at your main Twitter page'—and two, that you do deep research. You are not just looking at the company's website, but you are looking at how the company is communicating on all of their social media. This is especially good messaging for relaunchers worried that they are perceived as too old."

Kawasaki says she advises her clients to get their feet wet on Twitter by following companies and then tagging respected figures or experts in the field. "As they develop their area of interest and figure out who the thought leaders are, we teach them how to reach out and tag thought leaders or say, 'I read this article' and tag the author. Twitter offers a great chance to establish connections with people you otherwise could not." (Tag someone on Twitter with an @[TheirUserName].)

Instagram can also be a part of your digital brand building and research. Particularly if you're in a visual field, this is where you'll find your context—and Instagram accounts reveal a lot about corporate culture. Just like Twitter and LinkedIn, you can jump into a conversation and build connections by commenting.

Facebook can also be useful in your reinvention plan. Find Groups in your area of interest by searching keywords in the search bar on Facebook, and then jump in and comment on existing threads.

YouTube. "Don't forget about YouTube," Cohen advises. "Some companies have vast libraries of YouTube videos, and you could watch one and comment on it just as you would on a post on Twitter or the company's Facebook page or LinkedIn page."

It is all about creating a new trail of digital breadcrumbs that will help establish your professional online brand.

Cultivating your digital presence and connecting with online communities—these are critical steps as you make yourself and your skills visible in the world of work. But nothing is more persuasive than *you*. So get ready to brush up your interviewing skills and make your pitch—in person.

10.

READY, SET . . .
APPLY FOR THE JOB

You've done your research and targeted an industry and a company (or companies). You've augmented your skills and networked. You've put together a polished résumé and are even back on LinkedIn! You're ready to apply. But where exactly is that ideal job posting? And how do you make sure your résumé presents you in the best light for that job? How do you craft a cover letter that sells you by connecting the dots between your value and the job as well as finds a way to preempt any concerns the recruiter or HR team might have (time off, pivoting, looking at a more junior position)?

Ginny set up alerts on LinkedIn. She subscribed to the job listings in the House of Representatives and the Senate. She checked websites of think tanks and associations she'd identified. She set up alerts through Indeed.com. Just reading through the job postings gave her a good idea of what she might need to brush up on.

Laura found her job at GE through Indeed.com and applied through the HR system at GE. Even she'll admit she was lucky—the automated system had not been helpful during her search to that point. She'd submitted her résumé and cover letter through automated systems nearly twenty times already, and her résumé gap got her an automated rejection letter every time. The applicant tracking systems (ATS) that large employers use today are not your friend if you have a résumé gap or even if you are pivoting. If you don't fit the algorithm, you're automatically out.

So source jobs from everywhere, including places like Indeed .com, but then apply through the company website, which will always be more current than the job boards. Try to find a way to get your résumé to a real person. If you find the job on LinkedIn, the HR person handling the search is usually listed. Or if the job description says the position reports to the head of sales, you might be able to find that person on LinkedIn and submit a cover letter and résumé to them directly. In the best-case scenario a member of your network will work at the company and can tell you who the hiring manager is or even forward your résumé personally. Remember that 80 percent of all jobs are secured through a connection. And employee referrals have the highest applicant-to-hire conversion rate: although only 7 percent of applicants apply through employee referrals, they account for 40 percent of all hires. Your best shot is to target companies that interest you, then develop a network of contacts in and around it.

Here are some places to start looking for jobs:

Company website. If you have a company or organization in mind, start with their website.

Job boards. Check out Flexjobs and Indeed.com. You can search by type of work and location. If there's nothing in your area, search "remote jobs." But one thing to note: *whenever you're applying for a job from a job board, double-check the company website to make sure it's still available.*

LinkedIn. Once your profile is in good shape, you can click a button to let recruiters know you're available with LinkedIn's "Let Recruiters Know You're Open" feature, which notifies recruiters who use the premium LinkedIn service that you are open to being approached. (This is so easy: when you're in your profile, below the "About" section you'll see "Your Dashboard" and, in it, the heading "Career Interests." You can flag yourself for recruiters right there.) You can also apply to be listed as a freelancer in one of the many categories with LinkedIn's ProFinder.

Industry networking groups. Join an industry networking group. Many list industry job openings.

The alumni career office at your alma mater. Many universities have career resources for alumni, even if you didn't graduate within the past few years. The Kellogg Business School at Northwestern, for example, has a team of ten that work with alums on career development.

An executive recruiter or headhunter. Word of mouth and referrals are a great way to source openings.

Organizations. Look at places like iRelaunch, ReBoot Accel, Apres Group, and Path Forward, which all have job boards and are great resources for midcareer internships, otherwise known as returnships . . .

Wait . . . what is a returnship?

Returnships are paid, midcareer, return-to-work programs created to draw talented and experienced professionals back into the workforce. These re-entry internship programs work just like an entry-level internship program, with the exception that they are always paid. The programs are for mid- to senior-level career professionals who took a minimum two-year career break.

Carol Fishman Cohen, cofounder of iRelaunch, has been working with companies for more than a decade to set up these midcareer internships, and she says that at first, companies were skeptical. Now, as an increasing number of companies seek to increase diversity and woo back professional women who have left the career track, they are knocking Cohen's door down to set up returnship programs for them. There are midcareer internship programs in the tech, finance, and accounting sectors as well as in media and entertainment, education, marketing, and more. These programs have a cohort of three to thirty people who begin at the same time and experience the transition back to work together, with support, updating, and professional development provided by the employer.

Cohen says the hiring rates of the programs iRelaunch monitors most closely average an impressive 83 percent—a win-win for the companies and for the returners.

The internships are set up with the intern either working on a project or working in a specific role for two to six months. The assignments are appropriate for mid- to senior-level professionals, and some of the orientation and professional development modules are customized for the experienced professional, says Cohen. Other components are part of a typical onboarding experience for new employees who did not take career breaks or are similar to offerings in the entry-level internship programs.

When the internship is over, the person could end up taking a job in the department where they were working on the project, or they could get hired in a different division, or they could get hired in an unrelated role. Cohen says some companies feel they are offering returning professionals a high-level professional development experience and that even if they don't get hired, they've had a milestone transitional experience that will help them get hired somewhere else.

For companies these programs lower the perceived risk of bringing on someone who is coming off of a career break because they can try out the person and don't have to make a decision until it's over. They give the participants a gradual and structured ramping-up platform. The internship allows the employer to base the permanent hiring decision on a work product and a longer opportunity to get to know a prospective employee instead of a short series of interviews.

The success demonstrated in the programs that iRelaunch's Cohen began has now inspired others, and today there are more than ninety paid return-to-work internship programs across the country and around the world. Companies including Accenture, Morgan Stanley, Ford Motor Company, Johnson & Johnson, IBM, Goldman Sachs, United Technologies, Northrop Grumman, Walmart, Deloitte, and J.P.Morgan offer programs for women (and men) who are transitioning back to the workplace. Companies like ReBoot Accel, the Mom Project, and Path Forward, among others, now work with companies to create their own in-house paid midcareer internships or run centrally administrated midcareer internship programs for groups of companies to participate in. (See the Resources section for more details.)

"Today we are seeing a proliferation of return-to-work programs because they are working," Cohen says. Her blue sky is "every company that has a scaled internship program should have a scaled returnship program running side by side." And then, she says, they can broaden those programs to reach out to returning veterans, expats, and more. Think you might be a candidate? Take a look at the iRelaunch.com website for the full list of returnship programs around the globe and how you can apply.

And if you're an attorney who has taken a career break? The On-Ramp Fellowship is a centrally administrated year-long program matching attorneys who have taken a career break with law firms and legal departments in the United States. As of this writing there are thirty-one law firms that participate, as well as the legal departments at Amazon, American Express, Microsoft, 3M, Salesforce, Accenture, BMO, TriNet, and Trusight. The programs and application process begin at different times. Check onrampfellowship.com for details on how to apply. (See the Resources section for more on this.)

Sounds great, but the company I am interested in does not offer a midcareer internship program and has concerns about my career break. Should I suggest they give me a shot as an intern?

iRelaunch's Cohen says you should—but maybe not call it an internship. If you are in an interview process where you feel that some of the people interviewing you are hung up on your career break, Cohen suggests you say something along the lines of: "I understand why your colleagues might be hesitant to hire me because of my eight-year career break, but what do you think about bringing me on for a special project or contract consulting role? That way you could see my work before you make a permanent hiring decision."

Some managers may not consider it, but, says Cohen, "it is a way to lower the perceived risk that they might attach to hiring someone coming off a career break. We've seen people get job opportunities that way." (For a list of return-to-work companies and where to find midcareer internships, see the Resources section.)

———

CONGRATULATIONS, you've identified a job posting you like! But wait, before you hit Send . . .

Tailor Your Résumé to the Job Description

As we mentioned in Chapter 7, you'll want to tailor your résumé to optimize it for each job you apply for. You can do that by ensuring that key words in the job description are also in your résumé. Then be sure to check it on jobscan.co to instantly see how well your résumé matches up to the description. It's easy: you just paste in the text of your résumé or upload a Word or PDF file, then paste the text of the job posting you're interested in. Jobscan will also suggest other well-matched jobs, and it can analyze how well your cover letter and LinkedIn profile match up to the job description.

I think I'm qualified, but what if I don't check all the boxes on the job description? I don't want to stretch the truth and over-tailor my résumé.

When you come across a job description that seems like a good fit but you may not be fully qualified, don't immediately give up. Many times the HR department writes a job description that is based on an ideal candidate—desired versus required qualifications. Never assume that all the bullet points are required. If you fill a lot of them and have skills that can complement the job, then apply. However, it's important to still be realistic: if they want fifteen years of experience in a field and you've got three, move on.

What do they mean by "cultural fit" in this job description?

When you are looking for a job, there are crafty ways that job descriptions are being written to mask ageism (which, of course, we point out again, is completely illegal). You may have already come across these sneaky, ageist code words: "digital native," "recent college graduate," "cultural fit," "five to seven years experience," and "energetic person sought for young company." These are some of the skating-on-the-edge phrases that AARP's Disrupt Aging flags as being used by employers who are looking for cheap help or think anyone over thirty-five can't hack it. Our advice? Ignore it. If you are interested in the job and feel you are a match for the job description, then apply. Let your excellent cover letter address any perceived concerns they might have.

Make Your Cover Letter Stand Out

When you identify a job posting, whether you get your résumé in either through the ATS or to a real, breathing human at a company, you will need a cover letter or email. Don't do a generic one. This is another opportunity to tell your story, pitch yourself, and show a company right away how—and why—you'd add value to their team.

Tell them why you love the company. "The best cover letters I've read are from people who have a passion for my company and can make that passion come to life on a page," says Kathyrn Minshew of The Muse. "[Say] what you'd do there . . . share one or two very specific ideas of what you might do once hired at the company. [Explain] why you are a culture fit, and show who you are by the tone, words, and level of formality you use." If it's an uber-corporate office? Keep it professional. A creative ad agency? Absolutely ditch the "I was excited to find this position" opener. "But by all means, if there are specific cultural references you can include, do. Is the place known for being the most dog-friendly company in your city? Say how much you and your golden retriever would like to join the team," says Kathryn.

If you've been on a career break, the cover letter is your opportunity to highlight the skills you've acquired during your time off and demonstrate how they apply in the industry you're pursuing. If you were president of the PTA, explain how that adds value. For example, if you have been running a volunteer organization, you have been managing and motivating people without the carrot of a salary. Explain why that's a good thing, says Tami Forman of Path Forward. Make the case why it would be great to have someone who has been able to use the power of persuasion and influence—versus authority—to get things done.

The Power of a Persuasive Cover Letter

After almost twenty years out of the paid workforce, Mary was ready to go back. She'd been a practicing attorney in commercial litigation at a blue-chip firm before off-ramping when she could only find daycare that closed at six, followed by a series of unreliable nannies. Going part time meant full-time work on a part-time salary, so in 1997 she quit. In 2016 she began looking for work—signing up for volunteer work at the DC probate center and then doing research for her brother, a criminal attorney. She loved being back in the swing of things, and her confidence began to grow. She updated her résumé with her recent experiences in the probate center and with her brother. She knew that returning to a law firm was not for her, so she began sending her résumé in through the job boards, using key words in her résumé and targeting her cover letters. She started working her networks and made it through an interview and three-hour exam with Bloomberg. Mary was told she was one of three finalists . . . and then she was ghosted, never hearing anything again.

Finally, she heard about a job at a public policy institute that she loved. She crafted a cover letter telling the hiring manager that she would be great for the job because she wanted to contribute in a meaningful way to an organization she believed in—and that the title and salary were not the motivating factors for her. The organization contacted her and interviewed her over the phone. "I really hit it off with the person I talked to." Mary got an interview because her cover letter got the hiring manager's attention by showing her passion for the organization's mission. She did well in her interviews and got the job.

Connecting the Dots in the Cover Letter

My friend Laura used her cover letter to express her enthusiasm and knowledge of the energy industry and the company she was applying for. She described her responsibilities from her previous jobs and how they connected to the job she was applying for:

Excerpt from
LAURA'S COMEBACK CAREER COVER LETTER

My work with PPL Corporation, a Fortune 500 electric and gas utility, gave me an appreciation for the many variables necessary to meet daily energy demands. For over twenty years I have witnessed a transformation of the electric industry as it makes strategic shifts toward investments in renewables, energy efficiency and storage, smart meters and grids, to name a few. We cannot rely only on wind, solar, and hydro; the scale must be balanced with the realization that fossil fuels in some form and quantity will continue to play a major role, especially if nuclear plants are retired.

With experience in both government relations and business development, I bring a dual perspective. I understand the intersection of policy and business decisions—that is, the importance of anticipating and preparing for legislative and regulatory issues confronting many strategic corporate business decisions and communicating these effectively. While I was with PPL's Federal Government Relations office I worked closely with senior leadership as well as specific business lines to develop, advance, and implement corporate objectives before key policymakers and agencies. I represented the company at industry associations and worked closely with external advisers and industry peers. One of my primary responsibilities was developing a strategy to address climate change and greenhouse emissions, working with both internal and external stakeholders. Prior to this I worked on mergers and acquisitions as well as greenfield development; managing legal, financial, and commercial teams; developing investment recommendations for senior leadership; and preparing presentations for the board of directors. I succeeded at all of these responsibilities in a fast-paced team environment.

SAMPLE COMEBACK CAREER COVER LETTER

Dear [Recruiter],

As a [fill in your brand here] and a supporter of [company/ organization], I am writing to express my great interest in [job/role]. I am applying for this position because I believe that my passion for [organization] and my commitment to [mission of organization or department or role] makes me an excellent candidate.

With experience in [field], I have a good grasp on [pain points/ challenges the organization faces]. My work includes [use bullet points to tell a few signature accomplishments that are related to the challenges facing the organization].

Prior to this, I [fill in more accomplishments and list any important expertise—public speaking, certifications, etc.].

If I got this job, I would [share a specific idea of what you might do to add value/solve a problem/address a challenge].

I hope to have the opportunity to speak with you in person about how I can be an asset to [organization].

Sincerely,

[your name]

SAMPLE COMEBACK CAREER COVER LETTER

How to Convince a Recruiter That You Are Okay
with a Junior-Level Role

FOR A RETURNER

Dear [Recruiter],

I am writing to express my great interest in [job/role] at [company/organization]. I am applying for this position because I believe that my passion for [organization] and my commitment to [mission of organization or department or role] makes me an excellent candidate.

I realize that the position you are hiring for may be a bit junior for me compared to my previous jobs in this field—and that's okay with me. I feel that taking a more junior-level role will be the best way for me to get back in after taking time out of the workforce to [raise my kids/take care of my ailing parents/spouse]. I've kept my skills up to date, and I believe that my experience will translate well into this role. I am less concerned about titles than I am about joining a company/organization like [organization] that I so deeply believe in and respect. I am confident that, given the opportunity, I could make a major impact and add value because of [fill in your skills that would add value to the company].

[Here you can get specific about your skills and accomplishments and how you would add value to the company.]

I hope to have the opportunity to speak with you in person about how I can be an asset to [organization].

Sincerely,

[your name]

SAMPLE COMEBACK CAREER COVER LETTER

How to Convince a Recruiter That You Are Okay with a Junior-Level Role

FOR A PIVOTER

Dear [Recruiter],

I am writing to express my great interest in [job/role] at [company/organization]. I am applying for this position because I believe that my passion for [organization] and my commitment to [mission of organization or department or role] makes me an excellent candidate.

I realize that the position you are hiring for may be a bit junior for me compared to my previous jobs in [the other field/industry]—and that's okay with me. I feel that taking a more junior-level role is the best way for me to get my foot in the door, to learn, and to prove myself. I've always been passionate about [organization] and am eager to transition from my work in [original industry]. I feel like there is overlap in these areas, such as [name areas where you have skills that are transferable]. However, I also realize that I have a learning curve, which is why I'm okay starting at this lower level. I am less concerned about titles than I am about joining a company/organization like [organization] that I so deeply believe in and respect. I am confident that, given the opportunity, I could make a major impact and add value because of [fill in your skills that would add value to the company].

[Here you can get specific about your skills and accomplishments and how they are transferable and how you would add value to the company.]

I hope to have the opportunity to speak with you in person about how I can be an asset to [organization].

Sincerely,

[your name]

Don't forget to proofread. Here are a few basics:

- Make sure you spell the person's name correctly.
- Double-check that you have their correct title.
- Spell the name of the company correctly.
- Leave out the exclamation points, emoticons or :).

If you are emailing, the cover letter should be in the body of the email, not an attachment—this helps ensure your pitch is read.

Following Up After You've Sent Your Résumé

Always follow up professionally and respectfully, generally after a week, say the coaches we talked to. Never express frustration or make demands, even when no one on the other end responds. Also be sure to vary your communication methods: send an email, and if you receive no response after a few days, try leaving a voicemail message next. Remember: people are busy, so you want to acknowledge this and express appreciation.

Kerry Strollo, the recruiter we spoke with, says that if the position has been filled, say, "I'm so glad that I made your connection. Thank you for your time. Is there any other position that you think I could apply for?" And, she says, ask, "Is it okay if I stay connected with you?" "A good recruiter will want that! Make a connection and start a friendship with the recruiter. If they are a good recruiter, they will want to build a network with you and find a home for you if you're good. They don't want to lose you."

Brace yourself for rejections. See if you can learn from any of them. Is there any feedback you can fold into your search? If you are getting what feels like a crazy amount of rejections and never even getting a call for an interview, go back to your trusted friends and former colleagues and get their feedback on your résumé, job targets, and cover letters. Maybe you are looking for the wrong job, or maybe your résumé is not targeted correctly. Don't be afraid of feedback, and don't throw in the towel.

Or have you been ghosted (like Mary)? It happens, and it is almost worse than a rejection—no closure! If, after a few follow-ups, you hear nothing, then move on. It all worked out for Mary, and it can for you too.

———

AGAIN, REMEMBER THAT the vast majority of jobs are not awarded to people who apply online. They go to people who have already been in touch with the company of interest. Apply online to HR if you must, but also see if you can get in touch with the hiring manager directly. Find someone at the company who can help you get the inside scoop on who is handling the job search. And then try to find someone who can put in a good word for you. Advance on all fronts.

Eventually you *will* get a call for that all-important interview.

11.

SHOW YOUR VALUE AND NAIL YOUR INTERVIEW

At my October 2017 Know Your Value conference in New York City something amazing and totally unexpected happened. My team had hired a speaker—a woman I had never heard of—who, they assured me, would be excellent. She'd talk about body language, they told me. "Great," I said. "We need that because women need guidance on presentation and the signals you send just by the way you hold yourself." So I trusted their judgement, and they hired her for the event. But I never expected to be blown away. This woman, Janine Driver, had the audience in the palm of her hand from the moment she walked in—from the back of the room. Although she was an expert, it wasn't like she was a big name for them. I'd had A-list celebrities and Washington power players on stage that day as well, but none of them captured the crowd like Janine. By the time she was done she'd left everything on the stage. I had never seen anything like it. She had the women in my audience laughing, sobbing, on their feet, engaging with their neighbors in body language exercises. It was incredible—and at the end of her presentation I was crying too. Who was this person?

Janine Driver, now my friend and an incredible motivational speaker, has her own reinvention story. She started out at the US Bureau of Alcohol, Tobacco and Firearms (ATF) identifying and decoding the nonverbal cues of criminals who traffic weapons. She quickly became known for her ability to sniff out a lie. By the time she was twenty-four she had become one of the bureau's youngest body language instructors, and for the next fifteen years she taught interviewing and deception detection courses to more than thirty thousand inspectors and agents.

But after all that time she felt like her skills had another purpose. Janine told us that this realization was her "blue-streak moment, something that changes the direction of your life." For Janine, who'd risen through the ranks at ATF and used her skills to outsmart gun runners and white-collar criminals, the next level—being a top supervisor—wasn't where she envisioned herself.

"I always felt that what I was supposed to do on this planet was bigger than what I was doing. I felt that I was there to get these skills and bring them somewhere else, but I didn't really know where," she told us. She made a plan and gave herself five years to reinvent her career. While still working her day job at ATF, Janine created a website called LyinTamer.com and shortly after that founded the Body Language Institute. She started working with business executives, corporations, law firms, and universities who wanted to know how to send and read body language in a negotiation or an interview. She taught detective skills to business people and promoted her deception-detecting skills. Her side hustle started to garner national recognition, landing her appearances on Fox and the *Today Show*. She told her skeptical ATF colleagues that one day she would be an inspirational speaker, and many of them scoffed at her. They told her she'd never make it on her own. But in 2008 she packed up her boxes and left—a year ahead of her self-imposed five-year deadline. Two years later she had a *New York Times* best-seller, *You Say More*

Than You Think: The 7-Day Plan for Using the New Body Language to Get What You Want, and her former ATF colleagues would join millions of others watching Janine share her body language–reading techniques on national TV. For those of us who relish the "how do you like me now" stories, this one is especially sweet.

Janine is now a top inspirational speaker, teaching people how to become more persuasive communicators, problem solvers, and negotiators. She reinvented and repurposed her skills from catching the bad guys to teaching the good guys who work in law, finance, HR, sales, and executive leadership how to read people and how to improve their own body language to help them at work, on a date, and even in parenting.

"We're all in the business of selling ourselves," says Janine. "If we want to be successful, we've got to learn how to build rapport. True rapport is about empathy. It's about understanding the other person so well that you can experience the world through their eyes. It is the ability to listen with sincerity, to understand their values and connect with their emotions, which builds respect and trust."

That day when I first met Janine she was able to read, understand, and connect with the audience in a matter of seconds. She won them over, and if they had been interviewing her for a job, she would have been hired on the spot. She knows that to build a connection with your audience—whether it's in an interview, at a sales meeting, or during a pitch to an investor—you need to get in that person's head and understand what they want and need.

After I was fired from CBS I struggled to present myself as a confident go-getter in my interviews and to connect and show that I was the right person for the job. It was not easy, especially as I was not walking in from a position of strength. The loop in my head kept saying, "You were fired" and "You'll never work in this industry again." In interviews I had a hard time making a convincing argument that I could fill the organization's needs.

As Janine says, you need to sell yourself in an interview, and that takes believing in yourself. Logically you know that if you've made it to the interview, it's probably because you have the necessary experience and skills—your résumé showed that and got you in the door. But how do you turn your negative self-talk into the kind of energy that wins people over?

Confidence and the ability to make that crucial connection come through preparation, role playing, and practice. I know that from interviewing people every day for the show. Sometimes a simple ten-minute interview takes hours of preparation. And, of course, connecting with my interviewee is critical for eliciting something beyond a rote response.

The same applies for a job interview.

"I tell my clients: you want to be overprepared," says coach Mary Beth Barrett-Newman. "The amount of work you are going to have to do to prepare for an interview today is so much more than before because there is so much competition and the interviews are much more in depth. If you are not willing to do it, someone else will be."

Many jobs today have multiple interviews—sometimes a dozen or more: group interviews, individual interviews, remote interviews by Skype. One returner in the financial industry told us she went through fifteen to twenty interviews for each position.

So don't wing it. Do your homework. Research the company and the people interviewing you. It is so easy to get information on organizations and people today. Move beyond the company website: look for press articles, social media mentions, and employer review sites. Know their products, mission, industry, and any community involvement they've done.

Ask the HR person the name of who will be interviewing you. Check their LinkedIn profiles, and look for media mentions. Search for any connection points—same school, hometown, sports team fan, social cause—that might give you something in common. You may feel a little stalker-ish doing this kind of background research, but in a world where everything is online, this kind of preparation is expected.

Then revisit your brand value and tailor it for this opportunity: practice your pitch and connect the dots between your value and what the company needs. Every interviewer wants to know: Why are you the best person for the job? You may be one of twenty people the company is talking to—what makes you better?

My friend Laura says that not only did she come prepared with the latest industry information but that she also had practiced talking about how her previous experiences and signature wins would apply to the company's current vision and challenges. "I went through my deals. I reviewed the notes I had taken at industry events I'd attended. I then assessed where my skills and background would add value."

Like Laura, you need to prepare stories that connect the dots between your experience and the value you bring. Think about challenges you have overcome or difficult management and team situations you have experienced. What was the problem? What was your action to address it? What were the results? And how might that experience be applied to this job?

And you're going to have to brag. As Speaker of the House, Nancy Pelosi says to candidates for office as well as candidates for jobs, "Show them your why." So many women are uncomfortable drawing attention to their accomplishments, but face it: your talents are the reason you're in the interview. You are there to explain to the hiring manager why you're the best candidate and help them build a case that will persuade others as well. Think about how to really get that signature-win story down and talk briefly about what you did that defines your value in a tangible way.

Speaker Pelosi—no stranger to signature wins herself—suggests you take your preparation one step further. Be ready to talk about not only your past successes but also your future ones: "I think it is important for us to always talk about not just our experience, because that's what we have done, but [also] what we *will* do. Your experience speaks to your capability, your judgement, your record of success, but I always advise women when they go into an interview, 'Don't just say you deserve this because you have done this, this, and this, or you'd be the best because of this, this, and this. Just show your vision. And your vision will speak to your excellence. It's a demonstration without saying, 'I'd be the best at this for these reasons—my background, my knowledge, my experience.' It says it in a different way. Don't talk about why you should have it. Talk about what you are going to do next, and that will be the most eloquent statement."

And don't just think about your biggest strengths; also know your biggest weaknesses. Ask yourself: What's the one question I hope they don't ask me? Whatever that question is, then come up with a really good answer and practice it.

Think about the three things you want the interviewer to know about you, coach Barrett-Newman advises her clients. "Have those front and center, and make sure they come out in your answers. If for some reason one isn't discussed, at the end of the interview the interviewer will typically ask if you have any other questions. You can say, 'We didn't talk about this earlier, but one of the things you might be interested in is . . .' And share it with the person."

Prepare to talk about the connection between the job and your skills and values, but find a way to do it that feels natural. Coach Barrett-Newman says some interviewees, in a rush to explain their qualifications, "come off a little strong—rushing at me like a fire-hose—which is a little off-putting." Practice walking the interviewer through your résumé and explaining why your background fits the job. Your goal is to "put the equal sign between what you've done and what the company is looking for," says Barrett-Newman.

Practice helps make your pitch more comfortable. Get your story down and practice for the interview—out loud with your phone.

If you are interviewing remotely, whether via phone screens or on a multiperson conference call, they can be done on a variety of platforms—Skype, Google Hangouts, Zoom, FaceTime. If you've never tried these services, make sure you do a test run well in advance. Understand how the platform works, test your technology beforehand, and know to always look at the camera lens. Check your surroundings and background to be sure there's no distracting clutter. Make sure the light is sufficient and flattering, and don't sit with your back to a bright window, or else you'll be silhouetted like someone out of the witness protection program. And finally, make sure you block off time when it will be quiet in the background. Put the dogs and kids somewhere else, and silence other apps on your phone.

If interviewing on your computer, the right camera angle is critical. Make sure you adjust your laptop camera to be more flattering. Try placing the video at eye level and make sure your head and shoulders (only) are visible—put it on a stack of books if you have to. And keep your laptop open to just slightly more than 90 degrees to achieve the most flattering facial effect while also avoiding a white orb of light glowering from a ceiling fixture if you have one. And, again, look at the camera lens, not the screen. That way, to the people you're interviewing with, you appear to be making eye contact. I strongly suggest practicing with a friend to make sure you've got it right before the interview.

Approach this web interview as if you are interviewing in person. No *Anchorman* business-on-top-party-on-the-bottom outfits. Dress professionally head to toe—you never know if you might need to stand up. And even if you think your outfit looks good, see how it looks on camera ahead of time. Ginny did an interview over Skype once in what she thought was a nice-looking tunic top and realized, much to her horror (and a little too late to do anything about it!), that on camera it looked like pajamas! It was a good lesson.

What to Wear

When you get that interview you will likely utter these words: I have nothing to wear. It may have been a while since you last had to dress for an office.

When Carol Cohen asked Ginny to speak at her iRelaunch Return to Work conference, Ginny panicked. Later, after the panic over speaking in front of six hundred people subsided, Ginny told me she then panicked all over again about what she would wear.

Her closet was quite full, and yet strangely, at the same time, it contained virtually nothing that would be remotely appropriate. She says most of her clothes fell into the categories of "beach, too small, gym, perfect if I was thirty again, dog walking, home alone, and absolutely not."

I've seen her closet, and it looked fine to me. But she had a different view.

According to LinkedIn, nearly half (46 percent) of interviewers eliminated a candidate because of unprofessional attire. Don't be fooled by Mark Zuckerberg and his gray T-shirts—you can't wear that to an interview. "If you are not sure about the dress code, always err on the formal side. If the stated dress code is business casual, dress more business-like than casual. You can always inject a dose of humor into the conversation if you find you are clearly overdressed for the interview," says Sheila Murphy of FlexProfessionals.

Interview dressing is a universal pain point: *What the heck am I going to wear to the interview/first meeting/first day/week on the job? What do they wear in that office? How do I blend and look like I would be a great addition to the team?* Presentation is everything in an interview. There is no avoiding this moment.

Here's what I think: work clothes should look good without being a distraction. They should make you feel confident. You should not have to think about them once you have them on—no tugging at hems, no trying to hold wrap dresses closed in the breeze (uh, been there), no wondering if your top is gaping and showing too much. After all, the right clothes have the power to transform you from the inside out.

Don't wait until the day of your interview to get your outfit ready. Go to your closet, see what you need. Do it *now*, not an hour before your interview. The best options are neutrals like black, navy, gray, and camel. A solid, nice-fitting sheath that hits just at or below the knee is a winner on almost every woman, any age, and for nearly any interview situation. You may or may not have noticed it on *Morning Joe*, but I have a dress that works for me and have had it made in about a dozen colors. It is professional, and I am comfortable in it. Make sure your potential outfit does not show VPL (visible panty lines) or cleavage. And don't just look at yourself standing in front of a mirror—test it while sitting down: How far up does that skirt hike? Then think about accessories: What about your shoes? Avoid open toes at most interviews—they are too casual, and if your pedicure and feet are not perfect . . . *seriously, yuck!* Instead, go for the closed pumps with heels between two and four inches, whatever height is most comfortable for you and allows you to walk naturally. You can show them your personal style later, once you have the job and have been at it for a while—after you prove yourself. For now keep it conservative and professional.

And make sure your style doesn't read "out of date." Laura was worried that her dated professional wardrobe might make her look like Elaine from *Seinfeld*. (Remember those shoulder pads and the

WORK STYLE WITH SARAH LAFLEUR
OF M.M.LAFLEUR

For some professional advice on the matter, we talked to Sarah LaFleur, the founder of M.M.LaFleur. A Tokyo native and Harvard grad, LaFleur had been working in the finance industry and was frustrated by her closet full of "blah pantsuits." Sarah and her partners at M.M. set out to make dressing for work fun and easy. They also wanted to rethink the shopping process, making it more efficient and pleasant. Their hashtag is #better thingstodo . . . than shop. Shopping is by appointment at one of the M.M. showrooms or online.

What are the elements of a can't-go-wrong interview outfit, including shoes?

"Your outfit should be the least interesting thing about you. What I mean by that is: you want to wear something that you look and feel great in but that won't need adjusting or otherwise distract from you. You want the interviewer to be focused on your ideas, not your outfit. Choose a fabric that is breathable and has some stretch. When I'm not sure, I choose a dress, which I often refer to as 'the adult onesie.' You don't have to worry about matching a top and a bottom—it's foolproof."

How should you dress for a business casual office?

"The goal is to come across as put together and capable. Even if you're not wearing a suit—that would be considered business formal—you want

big hair? That was Laura back in the day!) She went out and got a Theory suit. "It is what I am most comfortable in and, therefore, most confident in. And although I'd like to walk effortlessly in heels like Mika can, it's low pumps for me." Ginny feels most comfortable in M.M.LaFleur dresses and pantsuits—a simple, updated look. No a look that communicates, 'I've got this. You can trust me.' You can never go wrong with a pencil skirt and top, slacks, and a blouse, or a dress and an elegant cardigan. Remember, comfort is key: pick something that you're going to feel good in."

What is the advisable work hem length?

"What's advisable can vary widely from one office to another, but when in doubt, go for something that hits just at the knee. It's flattering on all body types, and it's conservative enough for most business formal cultures but not too stuffy for a more casual workplace. It's a safe bet."

What are your thoughts on age-appropriate dressing?

"No such thing. Having worked with a lot of customers, I know that older women often prefer to not show their arms, but does that mean that you *need* to hide them? Absolutely not. If you've got great arms, show them. Our professional stylists have heard and seen it all—and I think that's why our customers rely so much on them. They know all the tricks to help you play up your assets and to emphasize the areas you're comfortable showing. Our bodies change and evolve over time, and your favorite parts about your body might too. That's okay! There is always something to flaunt."

stilettos for her either. Remember ReBoot Accel's Beth Kawasaki's advice: "We don't have to read young, but we have to read current." Consider your peers—who among your social circle really seems to have it together? What are they doing right? What works and is comfortable for you? That's what will give you confidence.

The Interview: Game Day

First things first: be on time, which means be ten minutes early. As the saying goes, early is on time, on time is late, and late is, well, in this case, late means you won't get the job. More than three in five (63 percent) US interviewers eliminated a candidate after they arrived late. Leave yourself enough time for the unplanned. If you get there too early, you can sit in your car or go hang out in a coffee shop.

First impressions and last impressions are key. Getting there on time is major. And when you do arrive, even if you just ran thirty blocks or had to suffer through an afternoon with your teenager's guitar lessons, gain your composure and put on your best self. Project confidence, energy, and enthusiasm until the moment you are out the door. Show excitement for the work and interest in the job. Passion is powerful. How do you think *Morning Joe* would go if I sat back and didn't seem to care? Look at my Instagram videos where I am talking to people for just a few seconds about knowing their value. I always have energy—and the best interviews are when the interviewees have energy too, which shows that they believe what they are saying and care about the topic. Even worse than appearing too nervous is showing a lack of energy. Be excited. Show passion about the job and yourself.

That said, even the most confident or passionate people may feel nervous about being interviewed. The best thing you can do to overcome nerves is to be prepared.

You may find that the person interviewing you is decades younger than you are. Don't let it throw you off. If you're feeling a sudden stab of insecurity about your age on interview day, remind yourself that with age comes experience and judgement. Be proud to be the grown-up in the room. Our life experience should lead to a sense of power—we just need to tap into it.

Here are some quick tips from Janine Driver on how to communicate confidence and make a connection through body language.

In the waiting room, stop imploding. When you are looking at your phone, you are "imploding" in your body language. You are looking down, collapsing inward, making yourself small. Don't do it. Put the phone away twenty minutes before the interview.

When you stand, have good posture. Don't be rigid, and keep your arms by your sides.

Sit at an angle to the interviewer. One of the biggest mistakes in an interview is to sit directly opposite someone. This is how we play chess. It increases stress and anxiety for both the interviewee and interviewer. Instead, move the chair 30 degrees off center.

Keep your body language open. Don't cross your arms in front of you—that creates barriers. Crossing your legs is fine, but be careful if you're wearing a skirt or dress, as that might have you revealing too much.

Don't turtle. When you sit with your feet under the chair, you are a turtle pulling its body inside a shell. Make sure your feet are at least under your knees. You can sit with them to the side if you are in a skirt. Ideally, sit in the front third of your seat—you'll look like you're ready to take action.

Read your interviewer. Mirror and be in sync with their body language and tone (without coming across like a pesky kid sister).

Keep your hands visible. If you are at a table, keep your hands where they can be seen.

Use your hands. Talking with your hands is good. The most watched TED Talks feature speakers who use hand gestures, but be sure to keep them within the frame of your body. Anything beyond that comes across as out of control.

Make eye contact. You can make a connection better this way. Don't look down—that makes you look nervous and unprepared.

Smile. Smiling conveys confidence and helps build connection.

Tackling Tough Questions

"Tell Me About Yourself"

Chances are that will be one of the first questions, in addition to why you want this job. Just like Laura did, know how your strengths can fill a particular organization's needs—that's your most powerful tool for making your case. If you've done your homework, you know what challenges the organization is facing and can discuss how you can help.

Don't age yourself in your language and tone. In an interview avoid statements that age you, like, "Back when I worked in the industry" or "I'm probably dating myself, but . . ." Don't apologize for your age; instead, figure out how your (decades of) experience can be of value to them. "When asked to talk about your past work experience, don't say, 'Well, this is ancient history, but way back in 2001, when I was working at Xerox . . .'" says Carol Fishman Cohen. "Instead, talk about it as if it happened yesterday. Remember what's relevant is that you *had* the experience, *not when* you had it. Say, 'When I was at Xerox, we faced very similar customer challenges. Let me tell you about one of them.'" And then, Carol says, "Have a specific anecdote ready."

You'll feel more confident if, before the actual interview, you record yourself in a practice interview. Make sure you sound energetic, positive, and passionate. Your age is not within your control, but how you act, speak, and hold yourself is.

If you are a returner, lead with your interests today, and then you can weave in your break.

I spent ten years in strategic communications for a tech company. After my kids were born I paused my career. During my time off, I took a course/did pro bono work/developed an interest in

. . . and now I hope to combine my years of experience with my new interest . . .

If you were fired or laid off, keep it brief and be honest. If your company was bought out or restructured and you were collateral damage, say so. When I was fired and had to go on interviews, I did not even know why I had been fired. When I was asked about that very public information, I just repeated what I had been told—that I was no longer needed. I was careful not to disparage CBS or anyone there, and I tried to quickly pivot the conversation to what I could do for the organization interviewing me.

Again, it's normal to be nervous. "If you find yourself getting a bit flustered, pause and take a deep breath," says Tami Forman of Path Forward. "Say something like, 'As you can probably tell, I'm a bit nervous. This is an exciting opportunity, and I don't want to blow it. Would you mind if I answered that question again?' By acknowledging what the interviewer can plainly see—you are nervous!—you show confidence and self-awareness. The interviewer will almost certainly forget whatever you babbled prior and remember both your humility and the great answer that you'll be able to give when you've regained your composure."

"You're Overqualified"

If you are returning after a career break, you may be applying for a job that is a few levels below where you left. Even if you addressed it in your cover letter, questions about why you are lowballing yourself may come up in the interview. Try something along these lines:

I am eager to get back into the XYZ field, and I have purposefully targeted this role at this level. I know I can do an excellent job at it and deliver great results.

"About That Résumé Gap . . ."

If you're in an interview process and feel that hiring managers might be hung up on your career break, address it directly, then pivot to making your case:

> [ADDRESS IT DIRECTLY AND SUCCINCTLY] Yes, I took time off to raise my kids/care for my parent/spouse, and now I am ready and excited to get back to work.
>
> [THEN PIVOT] The work I did on XYZ project at Acme offered similar challenges to what your organization is facing. Here is how I successfully addressed these challenges . . .
>
> [AND BRING IT HOME] I feel that my experience with Acme, the work/education/certifications I have attained recently, and my passion for [the mission of the organization] make me a great fit for your team. I am confident that I could add value right away.

If the hiring manager still seems to have cold feet over your career break, iRelaunch's Cohen advises you suggest a project or consulting role.

> If my career break is a concern, what do you think about bringing me on for a special project or contract consulting role? That way you could see my work before you would have to make a permanent hiring decision.

If that does not work, at least you have put the idea in the hiring manager's head, and maybe when a short-term project comes up, they'll reach out to you. It can't hurt to try, right?

HOW TO DEAL WITH AGEIST QUESTIONS

Branding expert and chairman emeritus of top ad agency Deutsch Inc. Donny Deutsch suggests taking a more aggressive approach if questions come up that seem to imply you're past your prime. As an employer, he has a theory about how to hire the best people: he always looks for someone with the "hungry eye"—someone whose self-worth is on the line at this stage of their career. He told me, "If I was running my ad agency—let's say I'm looking for a creative director on Visa—I'm not going to get the guy who did American Express. He already did it—he busted out! I want the guy underneath him who's thinking, *I'm better than my boss and I just haven't proved it yet*."

No doubt most women making a midlife career transition feel like their self-worth is on the line, so the hungry eye isn't hard to project. Deutsch argues that if a fifty-something woman interviewed with him, presented excellent credentials, and said, "Look, my kids are grown. I'm as good as anybody fifteen years younger than me. I'm as good as any man in this position," that would get his attention. "I'd hire her 100 percent. That means she's better than somebody who still has a nine- and eleven-year-old at home and has to be home by six o'clock. Now she has the work ethic and the same flexibility as a kid who's coming out of college and has no life. That's redefining your viability."

I really think this is one of your strongest selling points—your enthusiasm, maturity, and that you don't have a ton of distractions like the thirty-somethings. Use Donny's hungry-eye approach!

Common Interview Questions

Here are some other common questions, according to experts we spoke with.

Tell me about your background.

This is where you offer a conversational narrative that outlines your work experience and skills and connects that to the current position. If you have time, you can throw in a few short details, such as interests and hobbies, that round you out as a person. Experts advise that you do not get into details of your family life, medical history, or professional flaws.

Why are you interested in working for [insert company name here]?

Don't say "because I need a job." Give them a reason to hire you. This is where you tell them what value you bring and why you are excited about working for the company, and where their values/mission align with yours.

Tell me what you know about the company.

Talk about the company's product or service, target market, and business model. Show that you have done deep research by bringing up a recent tweet or other social media post about the company. Show how what you are doing and have done is relevant to the company and the position you are seeking. Go beyond talking about obvious details, like that they are an investment firm.

What's your greatest strength?

Experts say you need to be specific on this: talk about a specific time when you collaborated with other departments to come up with a great product. Or be specific about meeting tight deadlines or balancing multiple projects.

What's your biggest weakness?
Stay away from "I'm a perfectionist." No one believes that answer. Instead, experts say, be honest: talk about something you have been working on and what you are doing to get better. Of course, make sure it's something that is not going to raise a red flag for the interviewer.

Where do you see yourself in five years?
Research this one and see where in the company/organization there may be opportunities to branch out. Talk about how you would grow within the department and help grow the business. Connect it to your skills and how you would achieve this. Don't say, "I see myself still doing this job"—that shows a lack of ambition.

Questions You Should Ask at a Job Interview

Just about every interviewer will ask if you have any questions. Have some. Ask about the company, the industry, and the position. Ask questions about how you can have an impact. According to a recent LinkedIn study, nearly half (41 percent) of hiring managers say that asking well-informed questions is one of their top qualifications for a candidate.

"What Types of People Thrive Here?"
Broader questions about the culture and what it's like to work there can tell you a lot about the company.

"What Do You Want Someone in This Role and/or at the Company to Deliver in the First Six Months?"
The questions you ask should show that you are enthusiastic about the role and that you're interested to learn more about how to be a top-level employee.

"According to My Research, at Your Company's Latest Shareholder Meeting..."

Ask a good question that shows you've done a deep dive. When you do this, you want to make sure they are timely questions that aren't easily answered by the company website and show that you've been reading about the company and thinking further about its goals. Remember how Laura was able to talk about the CEO's letter.

"Is There Anything That Concerns You About My Background Being a Fit for This Role?" or "Do You Have Any Concerns That I Can Address?"

This is an especially good question if you are feeling like your age, career break, or job pivot may be an issue. It allows you to tackle head-on any doubts that might be brewing in the interviewer's mind. Have answers prepared and practiced to address what you think their concerns may be.

Questions *Not* to Ask in an Interview

"This Position Is VP level, Correct?"

Sometimes we cringe at the thought of starting again from the bottom or a much lower level. Maybe you were a vice president and the thought of doing things you used to have assistants for churns your stomach. Romy Newman of Fairygodboss, the largest career community for women, says to be careful: this is a common mistake she's seen when interviewing relaunchers. "I've tried to hire some returners, and in interviewing them a common mistake I hear is that they say, 'I can't do that work. That's beneath me. I was a vice president before.' It's difficult for me to hear because I am usually doing the work that they say they can't do. The workplace has changed, and fewer people have assistants, as the workplace has become digi-tized. We're all doing everything."

"I'm Looking for a Position with Flexible Hours. Is This Position Necessarily Nine-to-Five?"

You should know in advance whether a position offers flexible hours. Questions like this in an interview can come across as demanding or entitled. You might blow it, especially if you're applying for a job that's usually filled by recent college grads. One of employers' big-gest hesitations about returners is that they are not ready to return to full-time work. Your goal is to convince them that someone who doesn't fit their usual profile will be an asset, not a liability.

"I Have a Big Vacation Planned. Will That Be a Problem?"

Hold off on the vacation and flex requests. People tend to put their cards on the table too soon. Asking questions about vacation is go-ing to make an interviewer think you're more interested in things that are not essential to the job itself. When you get the offer, that's the time to negotiate your PTO (paid time off), your start date, and any time off for a planned family vacation. The interview is your chance to make the case that you are the best candidate for the job and to get a full understanding of the job responsibilities. Don't put in stumbling blocks that don't need to be there.

Close Well

End things on a high note, no matter what happened during the in-terview. And always follow up with an email thank-you note within twenty-four hours. (Handwritten notes will not necessarily reach the recipient promptly—and you want to reinforce your interest and reconnect as soon as possible.) When you compose your thank-you email, be sure to reference something specific from your discussion or even include a link to an interesting article that is relevant to something you talked about during your interview.

> Thank you so much for the opportunity to interview. I know that I can make a positive contribution to XYZ organization, and I hope to have the chance to do so. I have included a link to a great article on the topic we discussed.

If you don't hear back for a few weeks, follow up in an email. If you find out the job went to someone else, ask whether there might be any other work—maybe projects or contract roles you could fill that would give the company a chance to evaluate your skills. Show that you are still interested in working for the organization/company and keep in touch with the recruiter.

———

THE BOTTOM LINE when it comes to interviewing is: practice, practice, practice. Learn as much as you possibly can about what the company needs, and then determine how your skills can fill those needs. Have your signature wins and your vision for how you'll succeed at the ready, and close well.

You can do this.

12.

THE RE-STARTING SALARY

How women negotiate is a fascination of mine, mostly because I was so bad at it for so long. I almost quit *Morning Joe* in my second year because I was paid so little that I couldn't afford an on-air wardrobe, and I couldn't manage to make an effective argument to the network brass that my pay should be equal to Joe's. Later I realized I wasn't the only woman struggling to figure out what her compensation should be and how to ask for it effectively.

But, as I like to say, knowing your value is also about knowing whenever your personal stock is up or down. In our rapidly changing economy you need to keep tabs on your value. If you are returning after a career break or just a layoff, you may need to play the long game. This can mean a pay cut, especially for returners. I knew that, after a year out, my stock was way down, and that's why I took a massive pay cut to get back in. My industry is brutally competitive. But I realized that low, freelance pay would not be forever. I knew I'd be able to work my way up.

MANY PEOPLE WORKING their way up or back in have felt the pinch in their pockets. In 2016 economist Michael Madowitz at the Center for American Progress created the Career Break Calculator to show the long-term effects of either working or staying home. His study focused on stay-at-home moms like Ginny, who had been out of the game for seven years while raising her children and then experienced a "downsized" career for eight years. Madowitz's Calculator figures out how much a parent will lose (or, in Ginny's case, has lost) in income, wage growth, and retirement assets and benefits based on their salary when they stop working and how long they plan to be out of the workforce. You can customize the calculator to account for your gender, age, how much you earn, how long you plan to be out of the workforce, and your retirement contributions. The potential income loss for an extended break is staggering.

According to Madowitz and the Center for American Progress, "After taking into account the potential wage growth and lost retirement savings over time, a parent who leaves the workforce loses up to four times their annual salary per year."

Did Ginny regret time with her kids? Not a bit. Did she regret the lost income? Absolutely. She would never be able to make up that income, but the question now was how to best position herself to earn as much as she could. How do you figure out what your dollar value is after a career break? How do you avoid undervaluing yourself and losing even more income? How do you avoid overvaluing yourself out of a job?

Play the Long Game If You're Able

Every situation is different, but for the first job back after a break or a pivot, sometimes the top priority is simply getting your foot in the door. Romy Newman, president and cofounder of Fairygodboss, says, "My advice would be in the first return job not to become very obsessed with compensation. . . . My personal belief is that you go in and show your value, and you can then command the price that you know you are worth. It can be difficult returning because the market has changed. You've been out, and it is hard to know exactly what your value is. I am a big proponent of having signature wins and highlighting them. So once you are back in the workplace and you've got a few signature wins under your belt, you are in a much stronger position to negotiate."

Think of this first job back or in a new field as a bridge. "The mindset you have to have is, *This is a journey, not a sprint,*" says coach Liz Bentley. "You could hop from an assistant at a small company to being COO, depending on how talented you are. Being an assistant for a year and getting an assistant's salary doesn't mean that you will be there the rest of your life. The more talented you are—if you have a good education, had a good job previously, worked hard at your volunteer jobs, and have the skill set—the world's your oyster. Everything goes back to your own talent, your willingness to work hard, your own mindset. How hard are you willing to work? How much are you willing to adapt? How much are you going to put in once you get in there?" Bentley says she sees a lot of women who are very bright and talented, who have advanced degrees and have held big jobs. Women who have taken career breaks and who have been using their skills on PTAs and running clubs, events, or nonprofits. She says sometimes it's hard for them to accept the pay cut—and lower title—that they have to take. But "until they get traction in the job market and have a chance to prove their value, their value in the marketplace is zero," Bentley says.

It's important to know—and play—your long game. Does this opportunity, despite the pay being not what you're hoping for, help you move toward what your career vision is for yourself in two, five, or ten years down the road? This is not necessarily your forever job. "Sometimes just getting back into the game and working for a couple of years before pivoting into the job you really wanted is a perfectly good strategy," says career coach Carroll Welch. Keep that in mind as well when you are considering salary. "In general you have to strike the right balance between not grossly undercutting yourself and seizing a great opportunity to relaunch, even if the pay is lower than you'd wanted."

This is what Ginny did when she started writing for my website and working on the book with me. It was definitely not about the money, but it was a bridge back to communications and marketing work for her.

Sometimes there aren't a lot of options. After nine years as a stay-at-home mom, no savings, and a pending divorce, Donna did not have the luxury of time to find the perfect re-entry job. The newly single mom took what she could get—a job for $45,000, sixty miles from her home, which meant putting her children in daycare every day starting at 6:00 A.M. It was a brutal schedule and not a lot of money, but she looked at this first job back as a stepping stone and says it opened doors to other jobs. A few years later she's moved to a new—better-compensated and better-located—job. She says, "I'm now in a really good spot. I'm writing for a small, inbound marketing agency. I own my own home. I'm out of debt. My kids are doing great, and I have savings in the bank."

How Much Should You Be Paid for That Job?
Do Some Research

Knowledge is power. It is relatively simple to figure out salary ranges for different jobs, even if they are not listed in the job posting. Great websites for researching companies and salaries in various industries are Fairygodboss.com, Comparably.com, and Glassdoor.com. If you are interviewing at a nonprofit, you can look up their Form 990, which lists the salaries of the top executives. Take factors into consideration, like the company's size, the industry, and the location. When you get an offer, you'll want to know if it aligns with what that job's worth in the market.

Congratulations!
You Got an Offer—Now What?

This is beyond exciting for anyone who has been unemployed, underemployed, or on the wrong career track for a few years. And, naturally, many of us fear that the offer will disappear if we ask for a few days to consider. It won't. Career coach Mary Beth Barrett-Newman says to get all the information—salary, title, who you will report to, benefits, paid time off—and then ask for a few days to think things over. Make sure you get it in writing and that you have everything you need so you can look at it as a whole. She suggests something like this for your initial reply:

> Thank you so much for this offer. I am so excited about the opportunity to work at XYZ organization. Would you mind sending/emailing the offer package to me? I'd like to go through it, and I'll get back to you by [a few days from now].

"Then you go back and you really think about the things that are important to you," Barrett-Newman says. "Is it additional time off, is it some flexibility, is it compensation—maybe it's a little of each of those. And when you go back and you negotiate—start with the easier items, such as more vacation. Many companies now lump all time off together as 'paid time off' rather than separate vacation and sick time. Make sure you understand the definition. If you don't, now is the time to ask. Deal with negotiating any compensation components last."

Negotiating your salary and benefits is a normal part of the employment process, even if you've been out of the job market for a while. In fact, a study by Salary.com found that 84 percent of employers expect job applicants to negotiate salary when they receive a job offer. Studies also show—and my own experience backs this up, unfortunately—that women are much less likely than men to ask employers to improve their first offer. And if you think about the fact that subsequent raises are usually a percentage of the original number, you're likely to never catch up to the men who simply asked for more at the outset. So go ahead and ask. You have nothing to lose (except money—if you don't).

But you also need to balance the negotiation with the reality that you've been out of the job market for a while and the fact that your own stock is down. It's a fine line. The key is how you handle the ask. Come prepared—know your facts and numbers. Be able to articulate your own value. As I've learned, you can't get emotional and make it personal. And don't make it piecemeal. Do it all in one phone call or meeting.

When you have the conversation, start with the easy things: maybe you want to negotiate your start date or maybe you have a trip planned and need to ask for time off. Or maybe you are negotiating for more paid time off—say you want three weeks instead of two. As a midcareer hire, this is not an unusual ask. Get all those asks out of the way first, say the experts.

Then, if you are going to ask for more money, do it with facts to back up your ask:

From my market research I understand that this position in our region pays $60,000 to $70,000. You've offered me $58,000. I feel that with my recent certifications and my X years of experience I should be in the mid $60s. I would like to propose a starting salary of $65,000.

There are a lot of ways things can be negotiated, and it is all in how you ask for it. You don't need to come across as demanding. It does not have to be nasty. It can be positive and professional. Remember: if you take this job, you will be working with the person on the other end of that phone. Don't burn your bridges before you even begin. Do your research, and make sure that what you are asking for is reasonable. Keep your tone pleasant and professional. And make sure they can potentially say yes. In other words, if you are asking a nonprofit to pay you more than their executive director is paid, they cannot say yes.

And a Few Don'ts

Picture this: Your phone rings, and the caller ID shows it is the head of HR at Acme, where you've been through twelve interviews and you really, really want this job. You've been waiting for this call for weeks. You've been looking for a job for nine months, three weeks, and two days . . . and right now you are behind the wheel driving a car pool with six loud (and smelly) teenage boys on their way home from basketball practice *or* you are in line at Trader Joe's, helping bag your own groceries because you are helpful and there are twelve people in line behind you. This will take every bit of strength you have, but in either scenario you must let Acme's HR director go to voicemail. Don't take the call if you are not in a quiet place where you can answer professionally and have a discussion without distractions. The job offer will not disappear if you don't pick up the phone. Call Acme back when you can gather your thoughts in peace.

Don't turn down health—or any!—benefits, even if your spouse has them. But wait, you say: Won't they give me more money? No, the company won't increase your salary in trade for fewer benefits. Seriously, consider yourself lucky if this job comes with benefits, so don't give them away. And if your benefit-enhanced spouse loses their job (or you get a divorce, or worse), you'll be glad you have benefits through yours.

Don't negotiate unnecessarily. If it's a great offer, make sure you know the details, then take it! Don't be a jerk—recognize if an organization (say, a nonprofit) really can't offer you more money and don't push it.

And for Pete's sake, don't say you want to discuss the offer with your spouse. What guy says he wants to talk about it with his wife?

But if the job is exactly what you want and the money is what you are looking for and you have been waiting for so long for the offer, it's okay to not negotiate. We can still be friends. One of the returners we spoke with says she was just so beyond grateful and thrilled to have gotten the job and it was such a great offer that she just said yes. "I am just so eager to show up to work every day. I am so grateful for this opportunity with this great team and company. It was a great offer!" She's *still* doing her happy dance.

———

THE BOTTOM LINE is that you should know the job's value and understand that your current value could be down, but that it will improve. If you're transitioning and the job is right but the pay is low, just know that you will prove yourself and move up, and compensation will rise accordingly. But always do your homework first: if similar jobs seem to pay a lot more than what you're being offered, it's time to negotiate.

13.

GIGS, SIDE HUSTLES, AND MAKING IT ON YOUR OWN

Maybe you've done all your deep dives on yourself and on different jobs and have come to the conclusion that you really don't want to return to the grind of a corporate, fifty- to sixty-hour-a-week schedule. You want to control your own schedule and be your own boss. If it's about control, flexibility, and balance, piecing together gigs might be for you. Or maybe you've got an idea for a business, nonprofit, or consultancy and you think you want to go out on your own or with a partner. You're not alone—the number of women over fifty defining success on their own terms by starting new businesses is exploding.

Sometimes doing your own thing is about finding work that is meaningful to you. And sometimes the need for flexibility is about having time to find more meaning in life outside of work. "In my coaching practice I find that most people over fifty struggle to find purpose," says ReBoot Accel's Diane Flynn. "People with a sense of purpose live seven and a half years longer. Purpose has more impact than any other intervention, like working out, vitamins, or healthy eating. I believe it's why many women start their own entrepreneurial ventures, which provide meaning, flexibility, and social impact."

That happened with me, almost accidentally. I remember soon after *Know Your Value* was first published Joe and I were in New York City hosting a charity event. Afterward a group of young women rushed the stage. I assumed they were rushing to talk to Joe, but in fact they were all rushing for me. They were saying, "Please sign my book! I already used it and got a raise!" As I chatted with them I could tell that the experiences I had written about—all my vulnerabilities, failures, and successes as I learned how to advocate for myself—had resonated. It hit me that I could do more. This could be the teaching that I love to do. This was my purpose. I love teaching women how to do television; I'd been mentoring younger colleagues for years. And my message in book form was very similar: I wanted to help women learn how to communicate effectively—the technical and physical details, the gathering of data, how talent and intellectual ability can come through.

I remember leaving that event and thinking, *This is going to be my baby, my next passion.* It was as if the most incredible fork in the road had just appeared, and I had really found a path for myself. I decided to start a women's conference series. I put together the first one myself in Hartford, Connecticut, and invited female business leaders and CEOs to the table. Gayle King came to help moderate. The women in the audience were all on the edge of their seats, and I found that the event could even turn a profit—the message of the book translated to the stage was one I could sell. I really believed that this is something that I could grow and tweak, not just as a back-up job but as something of a mission. So, sort of unexpectedly, I founded a business, and I found my second purpose.

This is all to say that if you're not stoked about returning to or continuing with the corporate grind for whatever reason, I hear you. Let's talk about the other kinds of comeback careers that can light you up or simply pay the bills so you can find balance and time to pursue that long-lost passion.

Digging the Gig

When Ginny left Capitol Hill in 2001 the options for work were black and white: all in or all out. There was no easy way of finding part-time project work while she was home with children. These were the days of putting up flyers with tear-off tabs and finding freelance work through word of mouth. She was one of many highly qualified moms at home with kids who could have kept their skills current with fractional gigs. But the work world was not there yet.

Over the past couple of years that has changed radically. The combination of technology, a changed economy, and a generation—the Millennials, who refuse to be tethered to pretty much anything but their phone—today is revolutionizing labor for both employers and employees. Now, if you set up profiles on a few websites, you may be fielding project offers within days or even hours. It's like online dating meets work: swipe left if it's a dud and right if you think it might be your next love. Staffing companies have harnessed technology, combined it with the new landscape of work, and created user-friendly websites that aggregate flex, freelance, part-time, and project-based jobs with online screening, matching candidates with the right job.

Businesses that may not have been open to a remote or project-based workforce a decade ago are now looking for more flexible, "agile" workers they can tap into as needed to take over a project. Smaller businesses and startups can get the expertise of an experienced worker. And many workers of all ages and experience levels—especially women, who tend to be the primary caregivers to children and aging parents—are looking for flexibility, control over their schedule, a richer variety of challenges, and a way to acquire new skills and become the boss of their own careers or test-gig their way to entrepreneurship.

"What people want is changing," says Jonas Prising, chairman and CEO of ManpowerGroup. "They are working longer, learning more, and seeking a better balance between work and home. Not everyone wants to engage only as a full-time employee, and organizations don't always want that either."

Today it is estimated that anywhere from 22 to 36 percent of Americans participate in the "gig"—or freelance—economy. That is up from 10 percent in 2005, and a recent survey by Ranstad US, an HR service and staffing firm, predicted that half the US workforce will be employed in an agile capacity by 2025.

It's a trend that has exploded over the past decade for women who struggle to balance a traditional nine-to-six job with their family commitments. According to a recent study from Harvard University on so-called alternative work, from "2005 to 2015, the percentage of women who were employed in an alternative work arrangement more than doubled, rising from 8.3 percent to 17.0 percent."

"Until very recently women have had only two options: to lean in or opt out of the workplace," said Jenny Galluzzo, cofounder of TheSecondShift.com, a company that matches high-level, midcareer women with part-time, project, remote, or flexible work. "But today a growing number of us are refusing those limitations. Instead, we're remaking the rules and redefining what success means, using the gig economy as a promising third path that opens up options for time, balance, and flexibility."

Today's freelance is not just $25 blog-post articles and direct selling jewelry, especially for anyone with significant professional experience. Employers are recognizing that there is a top-tier talent pool available. As a result, experienced executives and highly skilled talent are finding high-value, short- and long-term gigs, from top executive and C-suite positions to interim COO and board memberships.

For anyone in a career transition, the gig offers a way out of something old, a way into something new, or an end in and of itself. Here's how gigging might work for you.

Gig jobs can provide an on-ramp back for returners. In the fall of 2015, after a ten-year career break from her ad agency days, Jill Grech dug out her 2004 résumé and started applying for jobs in content creation and marketing. The mom of three was eager to go back to work and hoping to find a position with flexibility. A few months into her search she heard about a new Chicago staffing agency called the Mom Project (for more, see the How to Find Gig Work box) and registered on the website. The Mom Project got in touch with her, and a month later she had a six-month contract working on marketing for a nonprofit. Word of mouth led to other contracts, and soon Jill was happily working fifty flexible hours a week for seven different companies. That contract work eventually became a bridge to a full-time position as the strategic digital marketing manager for a top university. For returners like Jill, project-based work may just be the résumé freshener they need to springboard back into the work force.

Gig jobs can be a bridge to solid ground after a job loss. Allison had been working in advertising for twenty years, fifteen of which she'd been with the same firm. That firm did not repay her loyalty; instead, on her forty-eighth birthday she was let go in the company's second reorganization in five years. She'd seen the writing on the wall and already submitted her profile to a few gig websites specializing in marketing. She's patched together a few short-term jobs, and although she's not making nearly as much as before, the gigs keep her résumé current as she looks for full-time employment.

If your experience is more like Allison's—maybe you've been laid off, restructured, downsized, or just decided it was time to leave— then gig jobs are both a soft landing and a bridge for you as you look for something more permanent. Firms like Second Shift, which

HOW TO FIND GIG WORK

Your Network

Find projects adjacent to your expertise by asking around, using your social network or LinkedIn. One gigger told us that once she had one project, word got out, and soon she had more than she could handle.

The Job Boards

There are the big freelance websites—Catalant, Upwork, Toptal, Flexjobs (see a more extensive list in the Resources section). You can set up profiles and alerts online.

And now there's a new breed of niche staffing companies that are geared specifically toward top-talent women (returning, pivoting, between jobs) who are looking for project-based or flexible job opportunities:

The Second Shift (thesecondshift.com)
A matchmaker of top-tier talent with remote, long-term, or limited-time jobs, the New York–based Second Shift pairs midcareer women with companies looking to hire for project-based work in finance, legal, private equity, tech, and marketing. Their jobs range from parental leave fill-ins to interim C-level roles, with the focus on projects that have some level of flexibility. Roles range from an ongoing project that requires three days in an office; to a six-month, full-time parental leave fill-in role; to full-time employment. Members have an average of ten years of expertise, and it's free to join but does charge a 5 percent fee per project.

value more recent experience (minimum ten years—see the How to Find Gig Work box), are a place to start.

Gig jobs can provide the holy grail of work-life balance. The proliferation and availability of gig work means that workers no

The Mom Project (themomproject.com)

The Chicago-based Mom Project now has more than seventy-five thousand members in its network, 30 percent of whom are women who have taken a career break and are looking to get back in. The flexibility and control are appealing. Search for and bid on jobs that are posted, and counter with different hours if the posted hours don't work for you. Candidates must have an undergraduate degree and five years of professional experience and must undergo an interview with a talent manager. The Mom Project's job board features "maternityships," temporary projects, and permanent jobs. It is free to join and apply for jobs.

Apres (apresgroup.com)

"Reconnect with your professional self" is the mantra of the New York City–based Apres Group. The digital recruiting platform connects women getting back into or pivoting within the workforce with companies that offer flexible work schedules and don't mind if you've had a career break. For a $49 annual fee you can access their job board, which has full-time, flexible, and return-to-work opportunities. Featured companies include Major League Baseball, Etsy, Facebook, Netflix, Memorial Sloane Kettering, and Microsoft.

Check out the Resources section for more project, flex, and freelance job boards.

longer need to choose between completely off-ramping and leaning in—they can keep a career oar in the water. They can set their own terms, have more control over their hours, pick up consulting work while they determine their next move, or make a career out of contracts. Working multitracks has an appeal to some who enjoy the variety of employers and challenges. It's a chance to check out an industry or company—to try before you buy or explore a career pivot without the full commitment.

But the romance of the hustle is not all it's cracked up to be. Gigging is not for everyone. It goes without saying that the income stream can be inconsistent, which leaves many people digging into their savings. However, if you are otherwise unemployed, it's better than nothing. And, of course, there are no benefits with most part-time, flexible, or freelance jobs, so if you are single or your spouse also gigs, then you'll be buying insurance out of your own pocket. What's more, figuring out details like how much to put aside for taxes can be challenging, and getting approved for a mortgage is impossible when lenders want to see consistent income from a steady employer. And sometimes flex is redefined as on-call, 24/7, when gig workers overbook themselves out of fear of not having future work.

The good news is that policy makers are beginning to recognize that the burgeoning freelance economy needs a safety net. Senator Mark Warner of Virginia has introduced legislation to create a new system of support for gig workers. And in the private sector, startups such as Icon, Steady, GreenLight, and Trupo are developing financial, retirement, and benefit products for gig-economy workers.

From Side Hustle to Startup

And then there's the dream. For many women at the midcareer stage there's always been the kernel of an idea of starting your own business. You've got a hobby, a passion, or an interest that you've been turning over in your mind for years. Maybe you've dreamt about opening a boutique or starting a consulting business or a nonprofit. For me, Know Your Value was the idea that became a book that became a side hustle that became my other career. There are plenty of people who have turned hobbies, passions, and side hustles into a full-time business. You can too.

It doesn't need to be huge. Being an entrepreneur doesn't mean you have to be the next Sara Blakely of Spanx—although that would be fabulous; it just means you have to find a need in the marketplace and innovate a product or service to address it. You may not invent the next shapewear must-have, but if your business pays the bills, lets you call the shots, gives you purpose and meaning and fulfillment, and has you jumping out of bed in the morning because you are excited about it, maybe that's good enough.

Sometimes you are starting your own thing because there's no alternative—the biases against career gaps or gendered ageism have closed too many doors. Lesley Jane Seymour says we all need a side hustle idea as a safety net: "My suggestion for women over forty-five is to think about something entrepreneurial. You need to have a reinvention plan in your back pocket. Not because of your inadequacies but because of the way the world is today. We don't know what's coming at us. Trying to waggle your way back into corporate life is really difficult. And it's not all it's cracked up to be, especially for women over fifty. You have to always have a real idea of what you might do if you had to do your own thing."

There are a lot of women leading the way and doing it after age fifty. Entrepreneurship is no longer just the realm of a bearded twenty-something tech guy in a T-shirt. Recent data show that an increasing number of women, from young moms to grand-moms, who want to control their schedules, pursue an interest, or be their own bosses are eschewing traditional corporate jobs and starting their own thing. In 2016 there were an estimated 11.3 million women-owned businesses in the United States. This is a 45 percent increase since 2007 and a rate five times faster than the national average, according to the 2016 State of Women-Owned Businesses Report from American Express. The report found that these women-owned businesses have provided nearly 9 million jobs and generated $1.6 trillion in revenue. Women of color were the biggest drivers of all of this, launching eight out of every ten women-owned businesses.

And in spite of the myth of that twenty-something guy founding a company in his dorm room, age is on your side. A study from MIT looked at data from about 2.7 million people who founded businesses between 2007 and 2014 that hired at least one employee. It found that the businesses with the highest rates of growth had an average founder age of forty-five.

Even if it means starting a business at the age your parents were retiring, you are in good company. A 2015 Kauffman Institute Index shows that the number of new entrepreneurs between the ages of fifty-five and sixty-four rose from 14.8 percent in 1997 to 25.8 percent in 2015. (Yes, we will all be working until we are eighty.) And, according to *Inc.*, the odds of succeeding in a new venture are in your favor if you have a few (or more) fine lines: a fifty-year-old entrepreneur is twice as likely to start a successful company as a thirty-year-old.

That's right: age—and the resilience, maturity, wisdom, pattern recognition, and networks that come with it—is a very big arrow in your quiver when it comes to starting a business.

Consider also that you may understand intimately the needs of a growing market. Worldwide there are now more people over sixty-five than under five, making the aging population the number-one biggest economic opportunity. Plus, women are the primary consumers in many categories. The market's getting bigger too: the number of people fifty-plus will continue to grow over the next decade to the tune of nineteen million, versus a growth of only six million for the eighteen-to-forty-nine population. What product or service do your fellow fifty-plus women need that you can do better than anyone? *Write it down now (before you forget)!*

But of course, starting a business or striking out on your own is risky, and if you need to make money right away, it may not be your best option—or, at least, you may need to keep it as a side hustle until you have the risk and financial tolerance to launch. Executive coach Liz Bentley knows this firsthand: "Here's what you should expect if you are starting a business, especially as a consultant: for 100 percent of the work you do your first year, expect to get paid for 25 percent of it. Expect roughly 75 percent of it to be done for free. The next year hope that [ratio improves] to fifty-fifty. And then the third year, potentially seventy-five to twenty-five." But, she says, if you make it through the first year, you learned from the experience, and it will get better. "Maybe the first year you're going to make $15,000. That's okay because you networked, you got yourself out there, you showed people what you do, you figured things out, you honed your product. Let's hope the next year you do better. Your goal is to grow every year. A lot of women don't know where to start, so they say, 'I love shoes. I'll open a shoe store.' Or, 'I like events. I will start an event planning business.' It can work every single time for every single person. They have to go in with the right mindset of what it takes the first three years of building a business to do that. It can work for 100 percent of the people—it's all about mindset," advises Bentley. "Are you willing to not make a lot of money in the beginning to hopefully make a lot more later?"

And of course, there are no corporate benefits. You'll be relying on your spouse's health insurance, or it will come out of your own pocket. There's no 401(k). And the "flex" part mostly translates to working round the clock. But you may not mind that if it's something you love to do—and that's one of the keys besides having the financial wherewithal: you will need to love what you do to make it work.

We wanted to know—besides passion for their venture—what it is that side hustlers should know before they quit their day jobs? And what advantages do we have as audacious women who've crossed the midlife rubicon when it comes to starting a new venture? Here's what I've learned and a few key things we found out from our round robin of experts and midlife entrepreneurs.

Don't Wing It:
Get Clarity with a Business-Model Canvas

With age comes common sense—and the knowledge that we might not want to wing it when it comes to starting a business. Good thinking. We want to be audacious, not reckless. Print out a template for a business-model canvas—a structured, one-page, nine-block template that helps you think things through when you are considering starting a new business. In many cases it has replaced the more formal, longer business plan. "Every startup needs a business-model canvas. Know what are you offering, why does it matter, how is it received, and how are you going to make money. Those are the key questions a business-model canvas answers," says Reboot Accel's Flynn: "Is it a premium? Is it a service? Is it advertising supported? Who is your customer? What are your channels of distribution? Revenue and cost structure?" Additionally, a business-model canvas will help you think through questions like: Can you deliver this service/ product profitably? How much will people pay for the service? What problem are you solving for them? What is your unique value proposition? What differentiates your business from the others? What are others charging, and how can you do it better? What advantages do you have over your competition or does your competition have over you? Or, if the revenue is coming through advertisers or partnerships, how will that work, and is it realistic? You can find sample business-model canvases online.

I didn't have a complete business model when I was starting Know Your Value, but I did conduct my own mini conference in Hartford, Connecticut. It was a bit of a test. I got my own sponsors, and the event made a small profit. I then sat down with the president of NBC News and MSNBC and pitched my passion about the event and how well it went and why it was a complete and total home run. And then I showed them the numbers—with the profit—and the rest is history.

Ginny's friend Kimberly Summers said she did key market research and homework on her new business concept before she launched a concierge service for boarding school students. The divorced mom had been working as a caregiver for Alzheimer's patients, but she had to quickly pivot to figure out how she could earn a living in a new town when her son was accepted into a boarding school far from home. Wanting to move near his school, she needed to come up with a way to earn a living in a new state and design her work around the September to May school schedule. She found there was a great need for a "mom in place of mom" for the boarding students whose parents are located out of state or internationally. Kimberly came up with the concept of catering to the long-distance families of the boarding school students, taking care of everything from allergy shots to birthday parties.

But first she had to see if her concept could work. Kimberly says she didn't do a formal canvas but instead did her research by meeting with the administrators at her son's boarding school to identify the need and to determine how her service would operate. She also met with other boarding schools in the area and determined that, indeed, there was a great need for this type of service. She spent a few months developing her platform with a web designer, and met with an attorney and with a mentor from a nonprofit women's business empowerment organization. She had the business up and running in six months. Kimberly's business, Student Concierge Services (scshereforyou.com), now has eight employees, and several other boarding schools in the area have picked it up. She is considering franchising it nationally.

Find a Niche Market No One Is Serving and Focus Group Your Idea

You may think that everyone wants your next shape-wear garment, but before you go and buy all that figure-perfecting nylon, do some research. "Until you get out there and really talk to potential customers, you actually have no idea whether there is a market for your product," says JJ Ramberg, founder of Goodpods and former host of MSNBC's *Your Business*. "So test your idea as much as you can. You can start with informal focus groups and online surveys. But—caution—be sure to include people beyond your close friends and family. Their desire to be supportive often colors the feedback they give you, and in this phase you need really honest feedback."

I found out big time that there was a market for Know Your Value when I wrote the book and got such a huge response. It turns out that no one was really addressing women about understanding and articulating their value. That first "test" conference in Hartford was sold out and had a waiting list, then we had people who walked in off the street and begged to come in. Women wanted to know more from those three words: Know Your Value. I also learned that putting on events is grueling work. It takes a strong, incredible team that believes in the mission. I have that, and my founding partners, Duby McDowell and Robyn Gengras, are still with me.

Sometimes you just need to go with your gut about what's needed, especially if what you are starting doesn't require a big commitment to launch. Two PTA mom friends stumbled into their own niche market when, on a bit of a whim, they started a little blog. "No one else was writing about this," say Mary Dell Harrington and Lisa Heffernan, the two women behind the powerhouse online community Grown and Flown. Back in 2011 the two suburban New York moms started commiserating about the fact that no one was writing about parenting in a way that spoke to them. "[Parenting advice] all kind of died out by the time your kid was twelve or thirteen, as if they didn't have any other parenting issues that they were facing," Mary Dell told Ginny.

Mary Dell had spent twenty years working for NBC, Discovery, and Lifetime, then took a decade off to raise her kids. Lisa had written three books, including the *New York Times* best-seller *Goldman Sachs: The Culture of Success*, and had also been a stay-at-home mom. But neither had ever started a website or blog. They asked Lisa's college-age son to help start the website.

They started a blog titled Grown and Flown, designed to help guide parents through the high school, college, and empty-nest years with real-life advice and pathos. They turned this simple idea into a massive online community. The site now shares guidance and stories on topics ranging from teen anxiety and depression to the college application process, bullying, and empty-nest syndrome. The two women have clearly tapped into something: in 2017 *People* magazine named them among the 25 Women Changing the World.

"We've experimented all along the way," adds Mary Dell. "We've been very self-taught. It's not like there was a playbook for how to make a site into a business. You have to get your content going and hope that as you grow you can get the business side going as well. You need to build a critical mass for a media company to have any value. It took a while for us to get the eyeballs. We offer advertisers or sponsors a new paradigm—a community—not just a business or a site. We just kind of figured it out as opportunities have presented themselves to us and as we sought out opportunities."

Today that "little blog" has a stable of 490 paid writers working on two or three new articles posting daily and 110 Facebook posts each week. The blog has attracted an interactive community of more than 350,000 parents across the country and advertisers knocking down their doors.

If Possible, Test Your Idea Out
Without a Big Investment

"Based on smaller-scale trials, you can get feedback, refine, iterate, improve, and pivot where necessary," says Flynn. "However, if your idea is a consultancy or service business, just go out and try it."

Jennifer Scherer tested out her business idea through a PTA auction. Scherer, who was a finalist at my Grow Your Value competition in 2017, had tried out a few business ideas—recyclable lunch boxes and using her psychology background to do market research—but her big idea happened accidentally. And she was able to test it out, refine, and improve it all through PTA fundraisers.

"It started out as a dinner group where I put together a kind of *Amazing Race* with people on teams, followed by dinner," she says. The team-building events would begin with a scavenger hunt around New York City and would end with a great meal. She did it just for fun the first time for a group of friends, but her friends enjoyed it so much that they suggested she auction off a dinner for a school fundraiser. "It made a decent amount of money, and then someone asked me to do it again. I kept on stepping it up with different themes and options, and it was raising thousands of dollars for these auctions. Then someone who was attending one of my events asked if I would consider doing one of these events for her company, NBC Sports." That first paid event in 2015 led to others at NBCUniversal, Citibank, NBC Sports, and Healthfirst. Jennifer now has a profitable event business—Magnified Events—with one full-time employee and about a dozen freelancers.

Jennifer offers these words of encouragement: "Find something that you're good at and figure out a way to make a business with it. If you just think outside the box, a lot of times there's a little business that can be had."

But what if you need seed money?

It Pays to Be "Mature": Use Your Old-Girl Networks for Resources

Female entrepreneurs start companies with 50 percent less capital than male entrepreneurs, according to research commissioned by the National Women's Business Council. People with experience mentor and give money to people like themselves, while those starting out do what they see people like themselves doing.

However, the advantage that women forty-five-plus have is networks. At this point in your life you probably have well-established connections to people who might invest in you—an advantage that the T-shirted twenty-something guy does not have. Put together that business-model canvas and start pitching your network.

When I pitch an investor, I get passionate. I dig deep. By the time I'm done with the pitch, the people at the other side of the table know that they have a partner who will roll up her sleeves and worry about every detail of the collaboration. I tell the story about the very first Know Your Value event in Hartford, Connecticut, and the women who got up on stage and pitched their value in front of a packed house. From the grandmother of sixteen from the north end of Hartford who wanted to open an animal sanctuary, to the fifty-something mom who was fired from her job on Wall Street, to the divorced mom from Avon, Connecticut, who wanted to open a gym in her basement, to the twenty-eight-year-old single mom who wanted to be the first person in her family to go to college. They learned that the pitch was critical. The woman from Wall Street won the event, but the twenty-eight-year-old single mom ended up being the real star of the day when the chief marketing officer from Bay Path University in Longmeadow, Massachusetts, stood up and grabbed the microphone and offered her a full-ride scholarship because her pitch was so effective. There was not a dry eye in the room, and I'm even welling up as I type this story right now. When I sell Know Your Value to possible partners, I tell the story of how it all began and how lives were changed, including mine. I pitch my passion, I dig deep, and I leave absolutely everything on the table!

Age is also an advantage when it comes to connections and support—you have a larger network than you did twenty years ago. Whether it's brick and mortar, consultancy, website . . . whatever—starting a business is hard. It helps to find a mentor, network with other local business owners, or start your own group of like-minded individuals. Ask your friends for help, advice, or connections. Create your own advisory board—after all, people think it's fun to be part of a startup.

The most powerful connections might just be with women who are in your same position. Best friends Tricia Sabatini and Stephanie Wright had both been searching for meaningful work after a few years as stay-at-home moms in Alexandria, Virginia. Tricia had a knack for making great chocolate-chip cookies, and Stephanie had always dreamed of starting an effective community-based social enterprise program. While training together for the Marine Corps Marathon in 2011, they came up with the concept of Together We Bake (TWB), a nonprofit that would be a comprehensive workforce training and personal development program to help at-risk women find employment and self-sufficiency.

The women say the partnership was critical as they worked to grow Tricia's small home-based chocolate-chip-cookie-baking business into a nationally recognized social enterprise program. In 2015 the White House recognized them as a Champion of Change for Expanding Fair Chance Opportunities. The women they help are returning to the community from the corrections system, facing long-term unemployment; some are experiencing homelessness, and some are recent immigrants. In 2016 they merged with Fruit-cycle, which made snacks from picked-over produce, and had hired employees through TWB. Each year TWB teaches four classes of women transferable workforce skills, like food safety and production, packaging, and business administration skills. The product line, which now includes granola, apple chips, and trail mix, is sold online and at local retailers, including Whole Foods. So far, more than 170 newly empowered and employable women have graduated from the program.

Tricia had some business experience running her home-based business, but Stephanie admits she had zero business experience. Neither had started or even worked in the administration of a human service organization, so their learning curve was significant. But they found help and support from the local community with finding space—a local church offered their kitchen. They got seed funding through an angel donor and friends and family. "We worked hard and had a true passion for the mission, program, and products we developed, so it made the work feel less like work and more like an adventure."

They strongly advise working with a friend: "There are so many benefits to working closely with a best friend. We know each other so well. We enjoy each other's company, and we care deeply about each other. Our strengths balance each other out fairly well, and we appreciate each other's integral contributions to the business. Our

---

GIRL POWER

There is a new crop of female accelerators and funding groups that has risen over the past few years, providing more resources for women entrepreneurs. From incubators and accelerators, boot camps and leadership trainings, there are more organizations than ever before connecting women entrepreneurs to investors and help. There is even a website, Alice (helloalice.com), that curates advice, connections, and even potential mentors for women entrepreneurs. (See the Resources section for more information.)

---

work is emotionally intense, so we are each other's cheerleaders and support."

Tap into Your Grown-Up Resiliency

You need to be able to get up when you are knocked down because you are going to hear "no" so many times or because you are simply going to mess up. This has happened to me countless times as I have expanded Know Your Value from book to conference to website. I really think that if I had encountered any of these problems at the age of thirty, I might have folded. But now, in my fifties, I think of these problems as learning experiences and challenges to overcome. Instead of wallowing in defeat, I move around the problems and just keep going.

Entrepreneur expert, Little Pim founder, and author Julia Pimsleur calls this having the "water around rocks mindset," and she says it is the key to entrepreneurship. If you are in your fifties or beyond, you probably have this mindset in spades because you've had to deal with so many challenges over the decades. "The mindset is critical. You have a vision. You are the holder and the keeper of that vision, and you will do what it takes to get to that vision, and you will bring lots of great people along with you. So any setbacks, anything that does not go well, any product launches that fail, any hires that don't work out, any money you lose along the way—it's not going to stop you. You might have to build a different mindset if your past experience is corporate America. As an entrepreneur, there's no roadmap, no bonuses, no public recognition for a long, long time. You have to be comfortable with risk. You have to be comfortable with delayed gratification."

Water around rocks also means you need to be ready to change your plan and be nimble. "Know your customer and be agile," says Alexandria, Virginia, women's clothing boutique owner Tamara Saltonstall. "Don't be too tied to your original plan, because it can change completely." The former interior designer who had learned to sew from her grandmother started out focused on her private label and custom designs but realized quickly that she needed to change course. She listened to customers and refined her offerings. Today TSALT, a fourteen-hundred-square-foot boutique, has nine employees and offers some of Tamara's own private label, less of the custom, and has added brands like Alice and Olivia as well as Frame and is moving $70,000 a month in merchandise.

Educate Yourself About Money Management and Systems

Don't get so focused on the fun part of your business that you forget about the systems. "Finance is the proverbial Achilles heel for entrepreneurs," says Pimsleur. "Business owners don't need to have a financial degree to run a business, but we do need to educate ourselves in order to create a cash runway, steward our money better, and raise capital." Ditto goes for the systems, like accounting insurance, legal, and employees, says Student Concierge Services' founder Kimberly Summers. "I have learned that when you set up temporary structures, instead of putting in the effort early on, it gets easy to rely on 'what works,' even when these systems may be highly inefficient or outdated. These areas are not necessarily an entrepreneur's bailiwick, so do not hesitate to put in a few dollars to have a professional establish good scaffolding. It is easier than trying to back-track and get a handle on past inefficiencies a few years down the line—and you will see a return on your investment."

———

GIGGING, doing the side hustle, or hanging your own shingle—so many women are proof that you can be the boss of your comeback career. Find your value, and share it with the world.

CONCLUSION

Ready for Takeoff

Talking to all the women in this book has been so inspiring to me and to Ginny. So many strong women are making major transitions in their careers and their lives.

Remember I mentioned in the introduction that I had thought that my career would be over in my forties—and how wrong I was? Working on this book, seeing my friend Laura and my sister-in-law Ginny go through their journeys, and reporting on so many other women has made me realize that not only can careers continue, grow, and flourish at fifty-plus but that careers can begin, relaunch, or reinvent at this age as well. Forty and beyond is not a career ender; it's a new beginning. This is your time to refuel, recalibrate, reboot, reinvent, and recreate your next decades—and rewrite society's narrative.

Laura, who is now back in the saddle after a thirteen-year break, showed me that time off the career track is not a career killer. I have never been happier to be proven wrong. She is successful proof of a new career paradigm that allows for a return after time off the career track.

As for Ginny, she took a big leap when she said yes back in 2016, joining me at Know Your Value and writing this book. Saying yes has given her a bridge back, and she is looking forward to returning to work in the world of politics and policy. This time she has a side hustle as she continues to fuel the progress of women like herself with their comeback careers. At the end of this journey she's learned to articulate her strengths and appreciate her passions—she now knows her "why." She can communicate her value proposition (just don't tell her it's a personal brand), she's on top of her digital footprint (thank goodness), and she knows how to lean in and give back to her network. Most of all, she's the first to call B.S. on ageism.

I hope at this point you feel armed for the exciting path ahead. You are done with excuses and self-imposed barriers. You know your strengths and how to talk about them. You know the challenges and how to handle them. And with any luck, you have some inspiration for your own journey.

That's not to say that there aren't real obstacles to overcome, as we all know. Gender discrimination is real. Ageism is real. Failure is sometimes inevitable, but it's also surmountable and makes you stronger and smarter. The disruption that the workforce has seen over the past decades will continue and accelerate, but that wave of change also creates so many new opportunities.

I say: just put one foot in front of the other. If you're considering a job change or if it's been thrust upon you, use this book, and make your plan. As women, we get things done. As Speaker Pelosi likes to say, "If you are a dreamer without a plan, it's a fantasy. If you are a dreamer with a plan, it's a victory."

So what is your plan? How do you plan to use the power of experience and knowledge that you've earned? Our age right now is about trading up—you are no longer a twenty- or thirty-something. But in place of that, you are stronger, wiser, and better.

Be the author of your next chapter. Ginny did that—literally—when she took on the challenge of writing a book with me. By saying yes to one project, she opened a bold new path for herself. She discovered that a frustration can spark a passion that can create a job or even a business.

Your comeback career may not be the easiest thing to do. In fact, it's never easy. It's never clean. And it never plays out exactly the way you expect. Some days may feel more like the Valentine's Day Massacre than Victory Day. The journey will require grit, determination, some sleepless nights, and a lot of work—not unlike your very first job—and in the end you may need to throw everything up in the air and start all over again. But, as I say, the hard knocks only make you tougher.

So don't just cruise. Have a game plan, and take back control. Say yes now to the opportunities you see—and those you make. Know your value . . . and your power.

ACKNOWLEDGMENTS

MIKA: Thanks to Ginny—coauthor, friend, and now resource to countless women who we will meet across the country as we help them own the fact that they are stronger, wiser, *and* better!

GINNY: Thanks to Mika for starting me on this journey, helping me see it through, and recognizing my value, even when I didn't. Thank you to Amanda Murray for always having the right words and helping me get this book over the finish line. And thanks to everyone who helped me along the way. I could not have done this without the incredible experts and thought leaders who generously took the time to talk with me and share their expertise and wisdom. A very special thanks to Carol Fishman Cohen and the team at iRelaunch for their help and all that they are doing to help women—and men!—return to work after a career break. Thanks to Diane Flynn and the team at ReBoot Accel and their advice and thoughts on career transitions for midlife women. Thanks to Liz Bentley, who, in talking to me about internal roadblocks and barriers we all face, made me recognize a few of my own. Thanks to my iRelaunch presentation partners, fabulous career coaches Carroll Welch and Mary Beth Barrett-Newman, who were always available to answer my questions. Thank you to Katie Fogarty, from whom I learned so much about branding and LinkedIn. Thank you to Lesley Jane Seymour for her insights and the important voice she has created for Boomer and Gen X women on CoveyClub.com. And thank you to all the women—like Laura and Alicia—who shared their own private stories, generously gave their advice, and allowed me to share their value with the world. Every day you're making the world a better place for all women. This book would never have been possible without you.

RESOURCES

Career-Finding Exercises, Programs, Methods, and Workshops

iRelaunch (iRelaunch.com) is the pioneer in the career re-entry space and has a comprehensive website geared toward women re-entering the workforce after a career break. They offer online guidance to help structure your return to work through the **iRelaunch Roadmap** as well as annual conferences and a full list of career re-entry programs.

ReBoot Accel (ReBootAccel.com) offers workshops on discernment (self-assessment), self-discovery, and finding your "why" and bootcamps for help with LinkedIn, résumé building, and interviewing.

Korn Ferry's program **KFAdvance.com** is a subscription-based service to help "move your career forward."

The Muse Grid. Found in *The New Rules of Work* by Alexandra Cavoulacos and Kathryn Minshew, it helps you "sift through, and narrow today's ever-growing menu of job and career options, using the simple step-by-step Muse Method."

The Landit Career Playbook (landit.com) is a "personalized playbook for women seeking to move their career forward." Find opportunities, create your personal brand, assemble your "board of advisors," and get advice.

Self-Assessment Tests and Surveys

Myers Briggs (MyersBriggs.org)
StrengthsFinder 2.0 (GallupStrengthsCenter.com)
Strong Interest Inventory test

Careerleader.com
O'Net Interest Profiler (mynextmove.org)
Passion Profiler (thepassionprofiler.com)

Career Coaching

Liz Bentley Associates (LizBentley.com)
Carroll Welch Consulting (CarrollWelchConsulting.com)
Mary-Beth Barrett-Newman, 2nd Career Consulting
    (2ndCareerConsulting.com)
Diane Flynn, ReBoot Accel (ReBootAccel.com)
Katie Fogarty and The Reboot Group (TheRebootGroup.com)
The coaches at iRelaunch (iRelaunch.com)
Advancing Women's Careers (AWCNY.com)
Chrissy Scivicque (EatYourCareer.com)

The Inside Scoop on Company Culture, Salary, Interview Questions, and More

Fairygodboss (Fairygodboss.com) is the largest career community for women and helps you get the inside scoop on pay, corporate culture, benefits, and work flexibility, with more than twenty-five thousand reviews by real women who work there.

Glassdoor (glassdoor.com) has reviews for more than six hundred thousand companies. Input a job, and Glassdoor will suggest "Featured Jobs," "Similar Companies," and a "Related Job Search" to help expand your search. In addition, Glassdoor has CEO approval ratings, salary reports, benefits reviews, salaries, and even office photos.

Strategic Volunteering and Social Purpose Websites

Catch a Fire (catchafire.org) begins by asking, "What are you good at?" Search by your skills and nonprofit causes. Use your "professional skills to make a difference" in project-based volunteering opportunities, from one-hour phone calls to three-month projects, all done remotely.

Taproot Foundation (taprootfoundation.org) connects skilled volunteers to nonprofits and social change organizations through one-day projects, six- to nine-month projects, or virtual opportunities.

Compass (compassprobono.org) assembles teams of MBAs and other highly skilled professionals to provide pro bono strategic guidance to nonprofits. (Locations in DC, Philadelphia, and Chicago.)

Idealist (idealist.org) lets you search volunteer opportunities as well as jobs and internships by keyword, skill or interest, and location.

Volunteer Match (volunteermatch.org) allows you to search volunteer opportunities by cause and location.

Encore (encore.org) is a program designed for people interested in transitioning to the social purpose sector.

Online Learning: Update Your Tech and Business Skills and Fill Knowledge Gaps

LinkedIn Learning is available to LinkedIn Premium members. It has webinars, videos, and online classes on business, creative, and technology topics. Check out tutorials in everything from project management and negotiation to leadership skills and online marketing strategy as well as learning about SEO, LinkedIn, spreadsheets, word processing, and more. Sample courses include Body Language for Leaders, Communicating with Confidence, and Writing to be Heard on LinkedIn. There is also LinkedIn Slideshare, a platform that hosts eighteen million presentations from experts on every professional topic imaginable.

MOOCs. A MOOC is a massive open online course that often can be audited at no charge. Two of the top academic MOOC providers are Coursera and edX, which both partner with universities to offer classes. In addition to free classes, Coursera and edX both offer paid "verified certificates" for successfully completing a course. Some MOOCs even offer college credit.

Coursera (coursera.org) has courses taught by "top instructors from the world's best universities and educational institutions." Courses include recorded video lectures, auto-graded and peer-reviewed assignments, and community discussion forums. When you complete a course you'll receive a sharable electronic course certificate. Coursera now also offers an iMBA. For example, there is a sample course in Design Thinking for Innovation (UVA).

edX (edX.org) offers courses from the "world's best universities and institutions to learners everywhere." edX now offers a MicroMasters degree in partnership with several universities. For example, a sample class is Critical Thinking and Problem-Solving (RIT/Rochester Institute of Technology online).

Udemy (udemy.com) offers sixty-five thousand online classes taught by experts that include topics in business, tech, and personal development. Sample classes include Make Your Writing Stand Out in 8 Easy Steps, Conquering the Fear of Public Speaking, and Introduction to Microsoft Excel for Absolute Beginners.

Codecademy (codecademy.com) helps you learn to code. Categories of classes include programming, web development, data science, and design. Learn a specific language like HTML, CSS, or Python, or learn how to design and build professional websites.

Alison (alison.com) offers knowledge and workplace skills training. For example, a sample course is Understanding Data Analysis and Reports in Google Analytics.

Skillshare (skillshare.com) is an online learning community with classes in design, business, tech, and more. Sample classes include Entrepreneurship: From Business Plan to Real World Success and Photoshop Fundamentals in One Hour.

The Muse (themuse.com) has a curated selection of online courses, including their own, in the categories of job search, business, marketing, and engineering and design. For example, a sample course is the Ultimate Job Search Course.

TED.com features talks on every topic imaginable, including Amy Cuddy on body language, Carol Fishman Cohen on returning to work after a career break, Anne-Marie Slaughter asking, "Can We All 'Have It All'?", and Sheryl Sandberg on "Why We Have Too Few Women Leaders."

Help with Public Speaking

Toastmasters International (toastmasters.org). iRelaunch's Carol Fishman Cohen swears by this international group in which members improve their speaking and leadership skills by attending one of the 15,900 clubs in 142 countries that make up the global network of meeting locations.

Websites with Résumé Help

SeekingSuccess.com
FlexProfessionalsLLC.com
TheMuse.com
JobScan.co

LinkedIn Help

The Reboot Group (TheRebootGroup.com). Founder Katie Fogarty helps individuals and businesses tell their story and create powerful professional identities.

Coworking Spaces

The Wing. the-wing.com (NY, DC, LA, San Francisco, Chicago, Boston, Seattle)
Hera Hub. herahub.com (San Diego, Carlsbad, DC, Phoenix, Atlanta, Seattle, Houston, Irvine)
The Riveter. theriveter.co (Seattle, LA, Austin, Dallas, Denver, Portland, Minneapolis, Atlanta)
RISE. riseworkspace.com (St. Louis)
The Coven. thecovenmpls.com (Minneapolis)
EvolveHer. evolveher.community (Chicago)
Paper Dolls. paperdolls.com (LA)
SheWorks Collective. sheworkscollective.com (NY)
The Hivery. thehivery.com (Mill Valley, CA)

Circle and Moon. circleandmoon.com (Roswell, GA)
Women in Kind. womeninkind.com (Denver)
Sesh Coworking. girlsesh.com (Houston)

Online Communities for Women Forty-Plus

CoveyClub.com
NextTribe.com
WeAreAgeist.com

Sourcing Jobs

The Biggest Job Websites

Indeed.com
Glassdoor.com
Monster.com
LinkedIn.com

Female-Focused Project, Part-Time, and Flexible-Work Websites and Clearinghouses

The Mom Project (themomproject.com) connects professionally accomplished women with world-class companies for rewarding employment opportunities.

The Second Shift (thesecondshift.com) connects seasoned, professional women who are looking for flexible, part-time, remote, or project-based work with companies that need help in finance, human resources, creative, business services, legal, private equity, tech, marketing, and more. Jobs include short-term projects, parental-leave fill-ins, part-time roles, and other flexible opportunities. Members have an average of ten years expertise in their field. Free to join, with a 5 percent fee per project.

Inkwell (inkwell.co). Founder and CEO Manon DeFelice started her company to connect talented moms (and other professionals too) with businesses and nonprofits for flexible work. DeFelice emphasizes that coming off a career break is not a barrier: "You may worry that you have been out of the workforce too long. We could not disagree more."

FlexProfessionals (FlexProfessionalsLLC.com). A niche recruiting and staffing firm that matches experienced professionals seeking meaningful part-time or flexible work with employers in need of top talent. With offices in the DC and Boston metro areas, FlexProfessionals also provides career re-entry programming and other job search support services to re-turners and other professionals who desire flexibility.

Apres (apresgroup.com). This digital recruiting platform connects women getting back into or pivoting within the workforce with compa-nies that "respect career breaks or allow flexibility." Featured companies include Major League Baseball, Etsy, Facebook, Netflix, Memorial Sloane Kettering, and Microsoft.

Freelance, Consulting, and Remote Job Boards

For Creatives
Behance (behance.net) is an online marketplace where creative types (an-imators, photographers, graphic designers, illustrators, etc.) can showcase their work and search for part-time jobs and freelance opportunities by location, company, or field.

99 Designs (99Designs.com) connects designers with freelance work— logo, website, book, merchandise, even tattoo designs. Compete for jobs and build a client base.

For MBAs and Top Credentialed Professionals
Catalant (gocatalant.com) is a marketplace that connects businesses to top-tier credentialed professionals for short-term business consulting proj-ects. Business development and sales, corporate strategy, finance, and HR are among the specialties.

An Emphasis on Screening the Jobs for You
Flexjobs.com is a screened and curated flex job board with jobs in catego-ries from accounting, legal, creative, nonprofit, to sales, and many more.

The Big Players in Freelance

Upwork (upwork.com). With a huge variety of projects across multiple categories, Upwork hosts jobs for web developers, designers, writers, accountants, sales, marketing pros, and more. Create a profile, and once it is approved, you have access to the job listings.

Freelancer (freelancer.com) is the world's largest freelancing and crowdsourcing marketplace by number of users and projects. After creating a free account, you can browse and bid on a limited number of jobs per month (a maximum of eight per month initially).

Guru (guru.com). With a worldwide talent base of 1.5 million, this site lists opportunities in professional categories, including engineering, website design, legal, programming, graphic design, business consulting, and administrative support.

Toptal (toptal.com) is a network of freelance software developers, designers, finance experts, product managers, and project managers.

LinkedIn Profinder is LinkedIn's marketplace of freelancers.

Sources for Midcareer Return-to-Work Programs

iRelaunch.com
OnRampFellowship.com
PathForward.org
ReBootAccel.com
TheMomProject.com

Entrepreneurial Help and Education

Alice (helloalice.com)
ReBoot Accel (ReBootAccel.com)
Million Dollar Women Masterclass (www.juliapimsleur.com/masterclass)
Rent the Runway Project Entrepreneur (projectentrepreneur.org)
Tory Burch Fellows Competition (ToryBurchFoundation.org)
Hello Fearless (hellofearless.com)
Women's Business Enterprise National Council (WBENC.org)

Funding for Female Entrepreneurs

Golden Seeds (goldenseeds.com)
Dreamit Athena (dreamit.com)
Astia (astia.org)
The Vinetta Project (vinettaproject.com)
Circular Summit (womeneffect.com)
37Angels.com
She Worx (sheworx.com)
Savor the Success (savorthesuccess.com)
Chic CEO (chic-ceo.com)
Ellevest (ellevest.com)
Ellevate Network (ellevatenetwork.com)
National Association of Women Business Owners (nawbo.org)

FURTHER READING

Aarons-Mele, Morra. *Hiding in the Bathroom: An Introvert's Roadmap to Getting Out There (When You'd Rather Stay In)* (HarperCollins, 2017).

Bolles, Richard N. *What Color Is Your Parachute 2019: A Practical Manual for Job-Hunters and Career-Changers* (Penguin Random House, 2018).

Burnett, Bill, and Dale Evans. *Designing Your Life: How to Build a Well-Lived, Joyful Life* (Alfred A. Knopf, 2016).

Burnison, Gary. *Lose the Résumé, Land the Job* (John Wiley and Sons, 2018).

Cavoulacos, Alexandra, and Kathryn Minshew. *The New Rules of Work: The Modern Playbook for Navigating Your Career* (Penguin Random House, 2017).

Cohen, Carol Fishman, and Vivian Steir Rabin. *Back on the Career Track: A Guide for Stay at Home Moms Who Want to Return to Work* (Hachette Book Group, 2007).

Comstock, Beth, with Tahl Raz. *Imagine It Forward: Courage, Creativity and the Power of Change* (BeeCom Media, 2018).

Conley, Chip. *Wisdom @ Work: The Making of a Modern Elder* (Penguin Random House, 2018).

Coughlin, Joseph F. *The Longevity Economy: Unlocking the World's Fastest-Growing, Most Misunderstood Market* (Hachette Book Group, 2017).

Driver, Janine. *You Say More Than You Think: A 7-Day Plan for Using the New Body Language to Get What You Want* (Random House, 2010).

Freedman, Mark. *The Big Shift: Navigating the New Stage Beyond Midlife* (Perseus Books Group, 2011).

Hagerty, Barbara Bradley. *Life Reimagined: The Science, Art, and Opportunity of Midlife* (Penguin Random House, 2016).

Heffernan, Lisa, and Mary Dell Harrington. *Grown and Flown: How to Support Your Teen, Stay Close as a Family, and Raise Independent Adults* (Flatiron Books, 2019).

Hoen, Tory, and Sarah LaFleur. *Wear to Work: A Guide to Building Your Ultimate Professional Uniform* (M.M. LaFleur, 2015).

Kay, Katty and Claire Shipman. *The Confidence Code: The Science and Art of Self-Assurance: What Women Should Know* (HarperCollins, 2014).

Licht, Aliza. *Leave Your Mark: Land Your Dream Job. Kill It in Your Career. Rock Social Media* (Hachette Book Group, 2015).

Lipman, Joanne. *That's What She Said: What Men Need to Know (and Women Need to Tell Them) About Working Together* (Harper Collins, 2018).

McNealy, Megan. *Reinvent the Wheel: How Top Leaders Leverage Well-Being for Success* (Nicolas Brealey, 2019).

Pauley, Jane. *Your Life Calling: Reimagining the Rest of Your Life* (Simon and Schuster, 2014).

Pimsleur, Julia. *Million Dollar Women: The Essential Guide for Female Entrepreneurs Who Want to Go Big* (Simon & Schuster Paperbacks, 2015).

Ramberg, JJ, with Lisa Everyone and Frank Silverstein. *It's Your Business: 183 Essential Tips That Will Transform Your Small Business* (Hachette Book Group, 2012).

Sachs, Wendy. *Fearless and Free: How Smart Women Pivot and Relaunch Their Careers* (AMACOM, 2017).

Shultz, Melissa. *From Mom to Me Again: How I Survived My First Empty Nest Year and Reinvented the Rest of My Life* (Sourcebooks, 2016).

Stromberg, Lisen. *Work Pause Thrive: How to Pause for Parenthood Without Killing Your Career* (BenBella Books, 2017).

INDEX